# BIBLICAL CHAOS
## HOLDING OPPOSITES TOGETHER IN TENSION

# BIBLICAL CHAOS

## HOLDING OPPOSITES TOGETHER IN TENSION

# James Kallas

Harmon Press

Biblical Chaos: Holding Opposites Together in Tension
by James Kallas

Copyright © 2012 by James Kallas.
All Rights Reserved. Worldwide.

Published by:
Harmon Press
Woodinville, WA 98077
http://www.harmonpress.com

ISBN: 9781935959267

Library of Congress Control Number: 2012932558

Cover Design by Harmon Press.

Darlean...
Partner in Pleasure and Pain

# CONTENTS

# Preface

There appears occasionally a book, which transforms the theological landscape, a book, which is so dramatically different from all that went before that it eradicates past research and sets up new parameters within which the gospel story must be seen. It renders everything earlier obsolete.

Such was Schweitzer's *Von Reimarus Zu Wrede.* (In English, *The Quest Of The Historical Jesus*[1]). The "theologians" of the late 1800s had sanitized Jesus, shorn from him all things supernatural.

The optimistic anthropology of evolution deemed man auto-perfectible, in no need of a Savior, wanting only a model, an example to emulate. And so Christianity was seen as an ethical code. Jesus was only a teacher, urging us to stay off newly seeded lawns and be nice to Negroes.

All that ended with The Quest. The emphasis switched from ethics to eschatology. New avenues of approach to the New Testament were forced upon us. There had appeared a book, which altered our parameters, erasing all of the assumptions that had gone before.

So also the same thing with Bultmann. Not a book but a

---

1. Albert Schweitzer and W. Montgomery, *The Quest of the Historical Jesus: A Critical Study of its Progress from Reimarus to Wrede* (New York: Macmillan, 1950).

brief article, the first sixteen pages of *Kerygma And Myth, A Theological Debate.*[2]

The article radically uprooted traditional understanding, which had stood for centuries. All earlier searches for exactitude of Scriptural meaning disappeared. No more debates over whether a Jesus-sentence was authentic or *vaticinia ex eventu.*[3] No longer a restructuring of the *sitz im leben* (setting in life). Precise definition of a specific Greek word ceased. For no longer was Scripture the final authority. The ultimate truth was no longer "Thus saith the Lord!" It was instead that which was acceptable, endorsed by the reason of emancipated man, that which was politically correct, deemed rational by the majority, not inspired words tumbling down from on high, which became truth. The article altered our parameters, sent us off in a new direction.

This present book is in that class. It is of that dimension. It will alter all that follows. It is not merely an alternate explanation of prevailing arguments. It imposes upon us a new yardstick, an entirely different set of benchmarks with which to measure the books of the Bible.

This is not a book on methodology, telling us how to hug homosexuals. It is not Sunday School pap. Nor is it one more tired monograph treating a too-often-visited minor topic. Its audience will be the serious New Testament scholar still convinced that intense concern for the literal meaning of the New Testament remains important. Its impact will be enormous. Why? Because it injects as central and formative a topic shunned or shushed for centuries.

The formative nature of apocalyptic is finally affirmed as the foundation of the earliest New Testament books. And the fact

2. Reginald H. Fuller, *Kerygma and Myth* (London,: S. P. C. K., 1953).

3. The term applied to a passage in the prophets or the gospels, which has the form of a prediction but is in fact written in the knowledge of the event having occurred.

that these motifs were later erased out of the later canonical books has not until now been made clear.

There are no books on the market similar to this one. The argument here is unique and ground breaking. It is unparalleled. Whereas others merely skirt the Satanic or deny it all together, this book forces us to face the fact that the dual apocalyptic emphases of Demonology-Eschatology were at the very heart of the thought of Paul and the utterances of the synoptics, and the erasure of these ideas in the late canonical books is what has produced Biblical Chaos.

Had the book ended there, that in itself would have been a service, obliging us to set aside all self-delusions about the insignificance of these motifs, seeing them only as a veneer able to be set aside without consequence. But the book does not end there. It goes on to make the stunning insistence that though the two ends of the New Testament are polar opposites, neither end is to be abandoned! Truth is found by holding opposites together in tension.

James Kallas
January 1, 2012
Thousand Oaks, California

Ω

## CHAPTER ONE

# THE NEW TESTAMENT IS BIPOLAR

The Gospel of John relentlessly and radically reverses the theology of Paul and the message of the synoptic Jesus. The Gospel of John is powerfully and persistently opposed to the basic worldview underlying those earlier New Testament writings. The New Testament is split asunder. The two halves are at odds with each other.

Differences between John and the others have always been noted. That is why the first three are called "synoptic," similar, to be seen together. But these differences have never been a major concern because scholars proceeded on the assumption that the clashes of content could be wall papered over and the differences reconciled.

A few of those differences *can* be reconciled. For example, Matthew, Mark, and Luke all agree that Jesus was baptized by John the Baptist. John hesitated to baptize Jesus, protesting that Jesus was superior to him (Mark 1:7, Matt. 4:14, Luke

3:15-16). But the very fact that Jesus knelt down before him suggested that the Baptist was superior to Jesus. It suggested that Jesus was only his disciple. When the Baptist was arrested and Jesus began to preach his same message, that further suggested that Jesus was only a continuator of the one before whom he had knelt. The Baptist was the prophet! Jesus only an echo. The Gospel of John had to erase such erroneous interpretations.

The fourth gospel had to erase them because Acts 19:1-7 indicates there were two types of baptism at Ephesus. One bestowed the Holy Spirit. The other was the water baptism of John the Baptist. This was not a clash between two different doorways into Christianity. *It was a clash between two rival religions!* One was the Christian religion, based upon Jesus as Savior and God. And in the other, the Baptist was the key figure! What a powerful propaganda weapon the proponents of the Baptist religion had! Jesus himself had knelt before the Baptist! Jesus was but an echo of his master's religion!

The Apostle John, living right there in Ephesus, erased such wrong views. He did so, first of all, by entirely eliminating Jesus' baptism! He refused to show Jesus kneeling before the Baptist ! Unlike the first three gospels, Jesus is never baptized in the fourth! Further, the fourth gospel flatly contradicts the synoptic view that Jesus preached only after John was arrested. John 3:24 insists that Jesus was preaching *before* John was arrested! Jesus was no echo!

The fourth gospel then goes on to enlarge and emphasize the hesitation the Baptist showed in the synoptics. It is only in the fourth gospel that the Baptist says of Jesus, "He must increase, but I must decrease," (John 3:30). John 1:19-23 puts the issue out of all doubt. Here, the Baptist emphatically insists he is not the answer, "I am not the Christ." He is not even a prophet! He is only a voice pointing to Jesus. Which he does twice in the very first chapter, two times identifying Jesus as the Lamb of God (John 1:29,36) and sending over two of his own disciples to follow Jesus (John 1:37).

There is no contradiction here. John is simply removing and reversing synoptic verses, which had opened the door to gross misunderstanding. He is correcting away from history. He is recasting what was said earlier only because the way it was said led to distortion.

Other so-called contradictions can also easily be dismissed and the four gospels harmonized. For example, if we had only Mark, we would have to conclude that Jesus' ministry lasted merely months. But in the fourth gospel there are three separate feasts of the Passover. The ministry of Jesus was not merely months! It lasted from two to four years!

Only a wooden-headed literalist can see this as a contradiction. John is simply supplementing Mark, adding to the narrative things Mark had skipped over. Mark is dominated by an air of urgency. The word ευθυς is used forty times, eight times in the first chapter alone. Because Mark writes with this sense of urgency, he overlooks or excludes many details. The gospel of John simply adds that which was earlier passed over.

The same thing can be said about the supposed conflict, where did the ministry of Jesus unroll? In the north or the south? Mark says one thing. It was in the north, Jesus did not go to Jerusalem until the final week of his life. But in John, Jerusalem is the central scene of Jesus' ministry. This so-called clash can be chilled by simply saying that John was merely adding on additional details passed over by Mark due to his dominating sense of urgency.

Because so many of these supposed contradictions can be erased or explained in this way, theology proceeded on the happy assumption that there really was no irreducible conflict between John and the earlier writings. All of the "contradictions" could be erased or explained, given sufficient extended energetic exegetical effort.

This happy assumption was reinforced by the fact that the life of Jesus in the synoptics and the one in John had so much in common. Both had Jesus raising someone from the dead. In John it was Lazarus, chapter 11. In Mark it was Jairus' daughter, chapter 5. Both told the story of Jesus multiplying the bread and feeding the multitude. In John 5:2-9 Jesus makes the lame to walk. The same happened in the synoptics. Thus the conclusion, which long prevailed, was that the earlier synoptics and the later fourth gospel, though they varied in detail, were cut from the same cloth and shared the same basic understanding of Jesus' ministry. Given time and continuing examination, it was naively assumed they could be harmonized for they said the same thing.

That happy assumption is now impossible. Major advances in recent New Testament studies have now brought us to the point where we must acknowledge an enormous chasm. It now must be recognized that John and the synoptics do indeed contradict each other in every significant area of theological importance.

The first of these *major advances* came with Schweitzer's *Von Reimarus Zu Wrede*.[1] Earlier, no one had ever made Eschatology the prime building block of Jesus' message. Jesus had been clinically sterilized. His divinity had been discarded. He was seen solely as a model to follow. Not sent to liberate an enslaved cosmos, he was only an ethical example, a human model to follow. That was all that optimistic evolutionary anthropology would allow. Every day in every way we were getting better all the time. All that was needed was a role model to imitate, and both John and the synoptics served up a Jesus sufficient for that purpose.

Schweitzer's *Quest* however altered the landscape. He rammed a new factor into New Testament studies. He argued

---

1. Albert Schweitzer and W. Montgomery, *The Quest of the Historical Jesus: A Critical Study of Its Progress from Reimarus to Wrede* (New York: Macmillan, 1950)..

that *Eschatology*, not ethics, was the formative factor in Jesus' life. With that, a key component of apocalyptic thought had entered in. That had never been done before. That factor was an extraordinary pivot point, demanding that everything earlier said had to be reevaluated.

That extraordinary pivot point, however, was almost immediately set aside. Schweitzer's advance was short-lived, almost stillborn. That was because Schweitzer overlooked one critical fact. It is difficult to criticize his stature and genius. He was a giant sailing uncharted waters. It is almost brutally unfair to say that he failed to see one of the shoals. But there *was* a flaw in his presentation. That is, he emphasized Eschatology in isolation. He wrote of it as if it were self-contained, an issue in itself, able to stand alone, discussed independently as if it had no roots or context. But Eschatology cannot stand alone. Eschatology had a root. Demonology.

*Eschatology* and *Demonology* are like Mr. and Mrs., they go together. They are like two blades of a scissors. Separated, they make no sense. The apocalyptic thinkers looked for the end of the world only because they were convinced there was something wrong with the present world! The planet was infected, diseased, enslaved under Satan. He was the source of all suffering and pain. There were only two alternatives. Either despair, we are helplessly overwhelmed. Or hope, God will set us free. And apocalyptic opted for hope! Eschatology was the conviction that God would end the tyranny of the usurping powers. *Eschatology did not exist in a vacuum.* No one would look for the end of the world if the present world were sound and sure!

But that is what Schweitzer did. He explained the life of Jesus in terms of Thorough Going Eschatology, which anticipated the end of the world. Schweitzer insisted that Jesus saw the end as imminent, about to explode in the immediate future. Yet Schweitzer ignored, never acknowledged, failed to pay homage to Demonology, upon which Eschatology was based.

That was the significance of C.H. Dodd's little book, *The Parables of the Kingdom*.[2] It was a book as powerful in its impact as was Schweitzer because it muted and negated all that Schweitzer had affirmed.

C.H. Dodd's aim was to refute Thorough Going Eschatology. *But he never attacked Eschatology as such!*[3] He never hit it head on! With brilliantly incisive logic, Dodd recognized that Eschatology all alone was absurd, without purpose or meaning. If the world was good and not infected, Eschatology would collapse. If the world was "divine," already under God's guidance, why end it? Thus, in his very first chapter, Dodd wrote of the *realism* of the parables and concludes that there was an inward affinity " between the natural order and the spiritual order…This sense of the *divineness of the natural order* is the major premise of all the parables, and it is the *point where Jesus differs most profoundly from the outlook of the Jewish apocalyptists*, with whose ideas he had on some sides much sympathy."[4]

By insisting on the untainted goodness of the present scene, by affirming the "divineness of the natural order," by denying any hint of Demonology, by refusing to recognize an infected cosmos, Dodd dealt the death blow to Eschatology! If the world is not septic, there is no need to cleanse it.

Once he denied Demonology, it was only an easy half step to deny Eschatology! He dismissed it as poetic language and not a concrete expectation. Thus, Dodd continued: "But these future tenses are *only an accommodation of language. There is no coming of the Son of Man 'after' his coming in Galilee and Jerusalem, whether soon or late,*[5] for there is no before and after

2. C. H. Dodd, *The Parables of the Kingdom* (London: Nisbet & Co. Ltd., 1935).

3. Ibid.

4. Ibid., 22.

5. Emphasis added.

in the eternal order. The kingdom of God in its full reality is not something, which will happen after other things have happened. It is that to which men awake when this order of time and space no longer limits their vision... 'The Day of the Son of Man' stands for the timeless fact.'"[6]

Once Demonology was denied, Schweitzer's profound forward step was lost. *Eschatology was internalized.* Dodd called it Realized Eschatology. Not a future event but an immediate happening. Instead of a *parousia*, a cosmic cleansing where the forces of evil would be hammered at last into submission, Eschatology was instead to be seen existentially, a psychological illumination, an internal religious experience.

(In passing, the extraordinary thing is that Dodd was right when he insisted that the Bible had a Realized Eschatology, an insistence that the cosmos was not enslaved but ruled by God alone! He would have been right, as we shall see (below, pages 50-51), he had been writing about John! But he claimed to have found it in the *synoptics*, where it definitely was not!).

Dodd was a calming balm, appreciatively received. It relieved the parish pastor and the professional theologian of having to deal with antiquated language of outmoded medieval thought. The scientifically sophisticated man of the modern age no longer had to be burdened with absurd images of demons distributing disease, of clashing angel forces descending from on high to fight a war of enormous dimension unparalleled in the past. Dodd's denial of demonology was a relief for many, indeed for most.

But there were a few, an unpersuaded minority, who feared that the failure to face Demonology and its consequent Eschatology might prove to be an impoverishment of the Christian message rather than a boon.

James Stewart wrote an article entitled "On A Neglected Element In New Testament Theology" and insisted that "...we

---

6. Dodd, *The Parables of the Kingdom*, 108.

have failed to take seriously the New Testament's concentration upon the demonic nature of the evil from which the world has to be redeemed. We have misunderstood as secondary and extraneous in the primitive Christian proclamation what in fact are integral and basic components of the gospel."[7]

T.S. Manson almost repeated those words when he wrote "the supernatural demonological element of the gospel is not a mere veneer. It is not a temporary trapping, which can be stripped away from the gospel. It is engrained in its very substance. It is needed to bring out its sense."[8]

That hesitating acknowledgement that perhaps Demonology was not peripheral but at the heart of things, set the stage for Rudolf Bultmann, no doubt the most influential voice of the twentieth century. Bultmann was a two-edged sword. He gave and he took away.

On the one hand, where Stewart and Manson (and MacGregor as well[9]) had only hesitantly suggested that the demonic and the consequent expectation of the end of the world might be more than a mere veneer, Bultmann went beyond hesitant suggestion and succinctly insisted that these ideas were the prime building blocks of everything that Jesus said and did!

His sentence, in Volume I, Part I, *Theology of the New Testament*, is the most comprehensive, profound, and powerful description of Jesus' unqualified endorsement of apocalyptic ever written. It is one of the most brilliantly insightful summaries ever penned: "Jesus' message is connected with the hope…which awaits salvation not from a miraculous change

---

7.   James Stewart, "On A Neglected Element In New Testament Thought," *Scottish Journal Of Theology* Vol. 4, (1951): 3.

8.   William Manson, "Principalities and Powers," *Bulletin of Studiorum Novi Testamenti Societas* III, (1952): 8.

9.   G.H.C. MacGregor, "Principalities and Powers," *New Testament Studies* Vol.1, (1954-55): 23.

in historical (political and social) conditions but from a cosmic catastrophe, which will do away with all conditions of the present world as it is. The presupposition of this hope is the pessimistic-dualistic view of the Satanic corruption of the total world-complex."[10]

That is what Bultmann_*gave*. It was at last recognized. It was no longer possible to deny. Jesus' world view was apocalyptic — Demonology and Eschatology dominated.

That was what he gave. But then Bultmann *took away*. He told us we could not take Jesus seriously! Jesus believed in demons, but modern man would not! To try and force modern man to accept such outmoded concepts and antiquated ideas would cost the church its audience. No one would listen. Therefore, his solution was, we had to rewrite the New Testament! Cleanse and update the language. Demythologize the message. Replace temporal Eschatology with the personal decision of existentialism. The end of the world was not to be seen as a future cosmic battle but as an immediate personal decision. The language of Satan and the horde of demons doing his will was to be replaced by the language of psychology: "…man is essentially a unity. He bears the sole responsibility for his own feeling, thinking and willing. He is not, as the New Testament regards him, the victim of a strange dichotomy which exposes him to the interference of powers outside himself…Although biology and psychology recognize that man is a highly dependent being, that does not mean that he has been handed over to powers outside of and distinct from himself."[11]

He came to the same conclusion as did Dodd, but what a difference! Dodd got there by saying apocalyptic ideas *were not there*, that they were foreign to Jesus. Bultmann, relentlessly

---

10. Rudolf Bultmann, *Theology of the New Testament* (New York: Scribner, 1951), 4-5.

11. Fuller, *Kerygma and Myth*, 6.

honest and far more insightful, said those ideas *were* there, were real to Jesus, crucial and foundational, but irrelevant to us today. So theology's task was to discard that which was clearly the underpinning of the synoptics and Paul, rewrite those early books, cleanse them of antiquated vocabulary, and use terms acceptable to the scientific sophisticate.

We have, elsewhere and often, rejected Bultmann's Demythologizing as a dead end danger, leading to nowhere. If we abandon Scripture as the final authority and replace it with what modern man might accept and what is politically correct and currently popular, we might retain our audience, but not for long for we will have nothing to tell them; we will have lost our message.

And so we are not going to rerun our anti-demythologizing diatribe. The only reason we mention Bultmann here is not to castigate him again for having castrated the gospel. Instead, we quoted him only to establish the fact that contemporary theology has at long last recognized Demonology and Eschatology. They are not peripheral asides. They are the quintessential building blocks of Jesus' message.

Once that is recognized, only then does it become apparent that John and the synoptics are incompatible, polar opposites. It is their attitude toward apocalyptic, which separates them. The synoptics and Paul affirm apocalyptic. It is the quarry from which they found the stones that form their base. But John is Realized Eschatology, denying Demonology and Eschatology. That is the purpose of this book — to lay bare the chasm separating the two ends of the New Testament.

*\*\*\**

The route we will follow to lay bare that chasm is this: we will begin by examining the Old Testament. A specific view of God emerges. He is sovereign and absolute, the author of all things. As such, suffering originates in him. It is a chastisement for wrong doing. There is no Demonology in the Old Testament. God is sovereign, the sole actor.

But that leads to a problem. If suffering is punishment for sin, why does a good man suffer? The Old Testament was unable to answer that question. That is why the Old Testament grinds to a cynical close, saturated with disillusionment and caustic chagrin.

After the Old Testament , things got worse. Under Antiochus Epiphanes, the exception became the rule. The *Principle of Retribution* was turned upside down. It was no longer the sinner who suffered. It was the elect of God, the noble ones who obeyed the law, who suffered. The conclusion apocalyptic came to was that the world was under Satan's sway. Demonology dominated apocalyptic. But God would restore his reign. God's rule would be re-established. His kingdom would come. Eschatology, the expectation of eventual liberation, was born.

That was the message of the synoptics and Paul. Demonology dominated, and Eschatology burned bright. The tyranny would end soon, and God's will once more would be done on earth as it is in heaven. The resurrection was the turning point in the war. The *parousia* would end it, the final victory.

The end did not come. Eschatology collapsed. The problem the Apostle John faced was to explain why Jesus had not returned. The conclusion he came to was that there was *no need* for Jesus to return! The world was already under God's control. John denies Eschatology and erases Demonology.

The synoptics and Paul, the earliest books of the New Testament, are apocalyptic, built on the twin cornerstones of Demonology and Eschatology. John radically rejects both. John and the synoptics cannot be harmonized.

We will conclude by showing that though the two ends of the New Testament disagree, it does not follow that the New Testament is invalid, or that one view must be minimized and the other alone emphasized. Biblical truth is paradoxical.

Truth is found by holding opposites together in tension. Even though the two thoughts cannot be harmonized, they must be held together, and proclaimed simultaneously.

Ω

## CHAPTER TWO

# THE OLD TESTAMENT
## GOD, SUFFERING, AND SATAN

The two major moments in Moses' life were the exodus and Sinai. The exodus showed that *God was strong*. Not all-powerful. That came later with Isaiah. But at least stronger than the god of the Egyptians, able to free his people from the fiery furnace of the Pharaoh. And Sinai showed that *God was holy*.

These two ideas were welded together into the *Principle of Retribution*. Be holy and God will use his power to bless you. Stray and you will pay.

The Principle dominates Deuteronomy. "O Israel, give heed to the statutes …that you may live" (Deut. 4:1). "The blessing if you obey…and the curse if you do not obey the commandments" (Deut. 11:26-28). "If you obey the voice of the Lord… God will set you high above all the nations of the earth…But if you will not obey…then all of these curses shall come upon you" (Deut. 28:1,15). "See, I have set before you this day life and good, death and evil…If you obey the commandments… you shall live and multiply and the Lord your God will bless you…But if your heart turns away…I declare…that you shall perish" (Deut. 30:15-17).

The *Principle of Retribution* not only dominates Deuteronomy. It is the key to every other Old Testament book as well. It makes sense out of Judges. When the people are faithful, they are blessed. When they become forgetful, an enemy arises. When they repent, God raises up a judge or deliverer. It makes sense out of Joshua. He says his house will serve the Lord, thus he is able to cross the Jordan and take Jericho.

The *Principle of Retribution* is the arch under which one walks when entering the piety of the Psalms. Psalm One is the classic expression of the *Principle of Retribution*. The first three verses deal with the good man who meditates on the law: "He is like a tree planted by streams of water, that yield its fruit in season, and its leaf does not wither. In all that he does he prospers." But the opposite is also true. The final three verses: "The wicked are not so…the way of the wicked shall perish."

The *Principle* is fine. The exception is the problem! Why does a good man suffer? How come an evil one often prospers?

Early on, exceptions posed no problem for there was no sense of individuality. The family or tribe, not the single person, was the unit. One could suffer for the sins of another family member. The sins of the father were inflicted even unto the fourth generation.

Or the affliction could be due to the invasion of a foreign tribe. Yahweh was obviously superior to the god of the Egyptians, but perhaps inferior to the god of the Assyrians; thus, they could do damage and make the innocent suffer.

Ezekiel did away with the first idea and Isaiah negated the second.

When the people blamed their woes on others in the family, Ezekiel rebuked them: "What do you mean by repeating this proverb...'The fathers have eaten sour grapes, and the children's teeth are set on edge?'...this proverb shall no longer be used...the soul that sins shall die" (Ezek.18:1-3). Ezekiel insisted that we stand before God as individuals, neither blessed for the virtues of others, nor punished in their stead for their wrong deeds.

And then Isaiah. When Assyria assumed substance and form and belched down from the north, wiping out ten of the twelve tribes, Isaiah said it was not due to the interference of a foreign deity. It was their own God who was responsible! He it was who called Assyria into action: "He will raise a signal for a nation afar off, and whistle for it from the ends of the earth, and lo, swiftly, speedily it comes" (Isaiah 5:26). Sennacherib did not act on his own. Sennacherib was only a servant. A non-knowing servant, but a servant nonetheless, for it was God himself who sent the Assyrians to punish his own people for having walked in the way of Jeroboam. "Ah, Assyria, the rod of my anger, the staff of my fury. Against a godless nation I send him, and against the people of my wrath I command him" (Isaiah 10:5).

The exodus is not the high water mark of the Old Testament. Isaiah is. It is Isaiah who hymns the sovereignty of the God of Israel and asserts the universal omnipotence of the Lord God of Israel. "In the year that King Uzziah died I saw the Lord sitting upon a throne, high and lifted up; and his train filled the temple. Above him stood the seraphim; each had six wings: with two he covered his face, and with two he covered his feet, and with two he flew. And one called to another and said: Holy, holy, holy is the Lord of hosts; and the whole earth is full of his glory'" (Isaiah 6:3).

It is Isaiah who sires the vision of God as omnipotent, omniscient, and omnipresent. He is a God of universal power, able to bend all nations unto his will. It is not only the earth, which is full of his glory. So also the heavens above. God is *sovereign*, but he is not sole, all alone upstairs. He is surrounded by a heavenly host, served by cherubim and seraphim, so many angels that they have to be divided into cadres overseen by archangels, the names of a few we know, Michael and Gabriel. The gods of the other nations are not denied. They are demoted. Their existence is acknowledged, but their impotence is affirmed.

One psalmist insists "There is none like thee among the gods, O Lord, nor are there any works like thine" (Psalm 86:8). Another adds "For great is the Lord, and greatly to be praised. He is to be feared above all gods" (Psalm 96:4). And yet another, "For I know that the Lord is great, and that our Lord is above all gods" (Psalm 135:5).

The Lord of Israel rules over these other celestial beings and summons them to conferences, calls council meetings, and there makes his judgments and gives them orders: "God has taken his place in the divine council, in the midst of the gods he holds his judgment" (Psalm 82:1). He is unchallenged, unmatched, he towers over this heavenly host: "…who among the heavenly beings is like the Lord, a God feared in the council of the holy ones, great and terrible above all that are around him" (Psalm 89:6-7).

God rules the world, *but he rules it indirectly*, exercising his authority via intermediaries. Among that celestial host there are angels whose task it is to manifest the protection of God, to pour out his blessings. These are the guardian angels. In Matt. 18:10 Jesus warns, "See to it that you do not despise these little ones, for I tell you that in heaven their angels always behold the face of my Father." Peter is rescued from prison, and concludes, "Now I am sure that the Lord has sent his angel and rescued me" (Acts 12:11).

Counterpoised to these *protective angels who express the love*

16

and compassion of God, there is *another group who express his displeasure.* In Egypt, God punishes Pharaoh for not letting the people go. The first born of every household is struck dead. It is the will of God, but the act is done indirectly through his servant, the angel of death, the destroyer: "For the Lord will pass through to slay the Egyptians…the Lord will pass over the door, and will not allow the destroyer to enter your houses or slay you" (Exodus 12:23). Note well, *though their task is destructive, they are loyal servants of God, executing only his will and not their own.*

This is where we meet Satan in the Old Testament. He is one of the heavenly host, one of the sons of God summoned to the council meetings of the holy ones. "Satan" is not a name, it is a title. It is a legal term meaning *adversary.*

In a courtroom, there are two lawyers present. One is the prosecutor, indicting, trying, and then punishing a perpetrator. The other is the advocate, the counselor seeking to protect the accused. Satan is the adversary, the legal arm of the heavenly council.

In the Old Testament, Satan is always a loyal servant, and he is also insignificant. He is mentioned only three times (Zech. 3:1, 1 Chron. 21:1, and Job 1:6-12). In 1 Chron. 21:1 his name is substituted for God's name in the parallel passage (2 Sam. 24:1) showing he was only an agent, as was the destroyer in Exodus 12:23. In Zech. 3:1, he does what a district attorney is supposed to do. He indicts Joshua the high priest. And that is what he does in Job. When God says that Job is a good man, Satan says that Job's piety is feigned merely to gain the blessings of God, and urges that Job be put on trial, which will prove his duplicity.

In the light of what Satan later became, one can perhaps see malignancy emerging. Perhaps an act earlier ascribed to God in 2 Samuel was later deemed unworthy of God, but it could be ascribed unto God's agent in 1Chronicles because the agent's sheen is already rubbing off. In Zechariah he is rebuked, his attack on Joshua is deemed extreme. And his accusation of Job proved to be unfair and unfounded. These things might indicate that he was on the brink of a metamorphosis unto evil.

Be that as it may, nonetheless it is abundantly clear, especially from the Job passage, that Satan never acts without God's permission! And he never goes further than God allows. *In the Old Testament, Satan is a loyal servant of God. There is no Demonology in the Old Testament.*

It is because there is no Demonology in the Old Testament, it is because God is all-powerful and omnipotent, towering over all, responsible for all things, that exceptions to the *Principle of Retribution* became increasingly troublesome. *They became the major problem of Hebrew religious thought.* Why does the good man suffer? How come? That was not the promise of Psalm 1:1-3. Why are there miscarriages of justice where evil ones prevail and prosper? That is in direct contradiction to what Deuteronomy said.

Two books wrestle with this problem. First, Habakkuk. He asks, "Why dost thou make me see wrongs…the law is slacked…justice never goes forth…the wicked surround the righteous, so justice goes forth perverted" (Hab. 1:3-4). He is told that the Chaldeans are being raised up to punish the perverse (Hab. 1:6). The *Chaldeans!* They are more vile than the ones they are coming to punish! That is no answer! It exacerbates his anxiety! And so Habakkuk protests: "Thou who art of purer eyes than to behold evil…why dost thou look on faithless men, and art silent when the wicked swallows up the man more righteous than he?" (Hab. 1:13).

Despite the empty senselessness of the answer, Habakkuk continues to trust in God: "Though the fig tree do not blossom…and there be no herd in the stalls, yet I will rejoice in the Lord" (Hab. 3:17-18).

Not so with Job. God himself confirms the goodness of Job

when he queries Satan: "Have you considered my servant Job, that there is none like him on earth, a blameless and upright man, who fears God and turns away from evil?" (Job 1:1, 8).

But the district attorney's task is to indict, not laud. "Satan answered the Lord, 'Does Job fear God for naught? Hast thou not put a hedge about him...put forth thy hand now, and touch all that he has, and he will curse thee to thy face."

God authorizes Satan to proceed: "Behold, all that he has is in your power, only upon himself do not put your hand" (Job 1:12). Given permission to proceed, Job loses everything —possessions, home, family, everything. Yet Job's integrity remains. Satan's accusation was inaccurate. He is, as God had said, a good man: "Then Job arose...and worshiped...the Lord gave and the Lord has taken away; blessed be the name of the Lord" (Job 1:20-21).

The problem is brilliantly laid bare. Here is a good man who suffers. Why does the good man suffer?

Chapter after chapter fails to provide an answer and so "patient" Job asks God head on in chapter 38 why this is so? And the answer is harsh. Job is told he is not bright enough to comprehend the mystery! He does not have the stature nor the capacity to comprehend suffering. He is not able to understand lesser things, such as where snow is stored in the winter, or from where the rain? Job is incapable of binding the chains of the Pleiades or loosing the cords of Orion. How then can he expect to understand things far more complicated?

Had the book ended there, that would have been sufficient. Not satisfactory but sufficient! Had God simply said — "Job, your legs are too short, your hat size is too small, you don't have the ability to grasp things like that! — that would have been a bitter answer, but acceptable, had the book ended there.

But the book did_not end there! Instead it went on to reaffirm the very Principle it had so magnificently exposed as inaccurate! In Job 42:10-12 we read, "the Lord restored the fortunes of Job…the Lord blessed the latter days of Job more than his beginning." *That is flat out nonsense.* The injured do not automatically and universally have their agonies erased and their fortunes restored! Life is not like that. Job is a bankrupt book.

Because the attempts to explain the exceptions failed, the later Old Testament books shudder with sarcasm and the canon grinds to an embittered close, a fact seldom given its due weight.

Some say Ecclesiastes expresses the orderliness of the creation, a time to plant, a time to reap, everything has its own time, all is in order. The exact opposite is its emphasis. It is not order but emptiness, which is underlined. "Vanity, vanity…" is better translated "Futility, futility…" Nothing makes sense. "I hated all my toil…I must leave it to the man who will come after me, and who knows whether he will be a wise man or a fool…this also is futility" (Eccl. 2:18-19).

That capsule of disillusionment at the folly of life is but prelude to the nadir, which comes in chapter 4: "Again I saw all the oppressions that are practiced under the sun. And behold the tears of the oppressed and they had no one to comfort them…And I thought the dead who are already dead more fortunate than the living who are still alive; but better than both is he who has never been, and has not seen the evil deeds that are done under the sun."

*That is a curse on life itself.* Because there is no answer to the problem of undeserved suffering, the Old Testament closes in cynicism. In the final book of the OT canon we read, "Where is the God of justice?" (Mal. 2:17). That is not a question. It is an accusation.

\*\*\*

That is the legacy of the Old Testament. Its ending assertions can be summed up in a very short list. One, there is despair because exceptions to the *Principle of Retribution* remain unexplained. But, Two, the Principle itself, though questioned, is never abandoned. Three, The Old Testament continues to insist that God is sovereign. All that unrolls is his will. Four, Satan dispenses pain, but Satan is only an insignificant servant, loyal, never acting beyond the limits imposed by God. Five, there is no Demonology in the Old Testament.

Ω

## CHAPTER THREE

# APOCALYPTIC LITERATURE:
# OLD TESTAMENT THEOLOGY REPUDIATED

First Maccabees tells us that the seeds of apocalyptic were sown by Alexander and the weeds came to full flower with Antiochus: "After Alexander, son of Philip the Macedonian… had defeated Darius…he fought many battles…and advanced to the ends of the earth…After Alexander had reigned twelve years, he died. Then, his officers began to rule each in his own place…From them came forth a sinful root, Antiochus Epiphanes, son of Antiochus the king" (1 Macc. 1:1-10).

The "many battles" he fought were of such heroic stature that he has ever since been called "The Great." But concentrating on his martial prowess camouflages his central impact. Alexander was not a soldier. He was an evangelist. He was a man driven by a dream.

Legend tells us that as a young boy he was tutored by

Aristotle in a cool cave of Pella. Aristotle was brewing tea while the student was doing his sums. The lad was startled when he heard the teacher exclaim, "We have found it!" When asked what had been found, Aristotle pointed to the bubbling water. When heated, water rose as a vapor and when it hit the cool surface above it was water again.

"We have found the secret of rainfall! When water is heated, it rises and when cooled, it condenses and falls! We have found the secret of rainfall! We no longer need live by ponds and streams, we can make the deserts bloom, all we have to do is build big fires!"

Apocryphal perhaps, but true nonetheless for it lays bare why Alexander "advanced to the ends of the earth." He was convinced that the mind of man was master of all. From Aristotle onward, he believed that human genius could harness nature and transform the world! That was why there were more cartographers and scientists marching with Alexander than there were hoplites and spear carriers. That is why he founded a city in Egypt, named it after himself, a city, which held the world's largest library! Hellenism was humanism, the Invictus conviction, the self-assured robust confidence that man could do all things.

"After Alexander had reigned twelve years, he died." But his dream never died. One of the *diodochoi*, Antiochus, one of the generals who ruled after him, had a descendent, Antiochus IV, who discarded his number and replaced it with a name. He called himself "Epiphanes," which, in Greek, meant "the light shining through." He was the light of the world.! He would share with the Semites the vision of Alexander. He would tell all those in his realm the glorious news of the majesty of man!

But when he tried, he was rebuffed. He found out fast that the Jews emphasized not the magnificence of man but the transcendence of God. "In the beginning, God created heaven and earth. *The earth is the Lord's* and the fullness thereof."

Antiochus Epiphanes saw that before he could plant he had to plow. He had to replace Hebrew ways so that Hellenism could take root. And thus it was that the man who deemed himself the light of the world produced the darkest night in Jewish history. They had known suffering before. Born in the furnace of Pharaoh, exiled unto Babylon, they had known pain. But never had anyone sought to rip out their soul, eradicate the roots of their religion.

"Then the king wrote to his whole kingdom that all should be one people, and that each should give up his customs… the king sent letters to Jerusalem…he directed them to follow customs strange to the land, to forbid burnt offerings and sacrifices…to defile the sanctuary…to sacrifice swine and unclean animals…so that all should forget the law…whoever does not obey the command of the king shall die" (1 Macc. 1:41-50).

After washing down the walls of the temple with pig blood, "The books of the law which they found they tore to pieces and burned with fire" (1 Macc. 1:56).

But nadir of the atrocities: "According to the decree, they put to death the women who had their children circumcised, and their families, and those who circumcised them; and they hung the infants from their mothers' necks" (1 Macc. 1;60-61).

The destructive violence is summed up in dramatic understatement: "And very great wrath came upon Israel" (1 Macc. 1:64).

\* \* \*

The savagery produced a new genre of literature, called apocalyptic. Such fiendish acts, defiling the temple, burning the word of God, hanging little babies around their dead mothers' necks where they would starve in putrefaction stench, led to only one conclusion. This was *not* the will of God! God would not do such things! It had, therefore, to be someone else! There had been a war in heaven. Some other than God, had gone berserk, and was ravaging the elect of God with brutality of an unprecedented dimension. On earth, *The Principle of Retribution* had been reversed. Everything was upside down. No longer did Psalm One ring true. The man whose "delight is in the law of the Lord, and on the law he meditates day and night" was no longer "like a tree planted by streams of water." No longer was it true that "In all that he does, he prospers." No longer was it true that "the way of the wicked will perish."

*Old Testament theology was repudiated.* The earth was no longer full of God's glory. Satan, already suspect in earlier writings, was the one who led the revolt. God had put down the revolt above, God's will was restored in heaven, upstairs all was put back in order, but Satan had been cast out, hurled down to earth, and there his rage was great. That was why "very great wrath came upon Israel."

The literature of the intertestamental period abounds with accounts of the fall of the angels. The revolt of the angels, their rebellion against God, their theft of this world, their tyranny of this world, their despising of God and their workings of evil in attacking the elect and corrupting the world of man is the near-universal theme of apocalyptic. The Book of Enoch has two separate accounts of the fall of the angels. The Book of Jubilees has its own account. In all of this literature, the evil nature of the fallen Satan is expounded. He is no longer the servant of God but an enemy. And since he rules this world, the world itself has taken on a malignant perverted strain.

The corrupted nature of the world is seen in such things as the worms in fruit, famines, the refusal of trees to bear fruit, storms at sea where the devil sweeps away countless helpless victims. All these evidences of a cosmos in revolt, of an enslaved physical world subject to the whims of a perverted enemy of God; all these are themes of apocalyptic literature.

It was a literature of persecution, but it was a literature of hope as well. Throbbing through the wretched ordeal of enormous pain, was the conviction that God would regain mastery. *Demonology produced Eschatology*! Heaven had been cleansed, so also his will would be done on earth. His kingdom would come, his will would once more be done. Satan would be vanquished.

But these evil ones were firmly entrenched; they ruled every corner of the world. Thus, when God came to drive them out, there would be a savage counterattack, utter chaos, a time of complete havoc and destruction. The demons were solidly planted, and as the kingdom of God drew near, they would fight to hold on to their stolen possessions. There would be a time of tribulation as had not been seen from the beginning of creation until then, for never before had cosmic figures of such dimension engaged in battle. The cosmos itself would be shaken, the sun darkened, the moon not giving its light, stars would be falling. But God would prevail.

The Essenes were a succinct summary of apocalyptic, a microcosm. They had no sex. If a husband and a wife came to the Qumran community, they separated, never saw each other again. Who would want to bring a child into a world ruled by Satan? They had no money. An abundance of wealth in a demon-controlled world would indicate only one thing, alliance with the evil one. Ascetic, living in the wilderness, almost no clothing, eating practically nothing but locusts and honey, they turned their backs on the wealth of the world.

Yet they were optimistic! They were convinced that God would act, God would rescue, God would redeem the Elect. The scroll most indicative of Essene thought was "The War Of The Sons Of Light And The Sons of Darkness." Its importance is reflected in the architecture of the structure in which the scrolls are today housed. One building is white, the other black. The scroll insisted: God would restore order! "One like unto a Son of Man" (having the appearance of a human being, but more, a divine redeemer) would lead the armies of light unto victory.

\* \* \*

Before we go any further, this has to be said. Judaism created apocalyptic literature, the belief in the fall of Satan and the corruption of the total world complex. But Judaism later abandoned such ideas. The apocalyptic books among the Apocrypha were never canonized, and this for two reasons.

First, politics. The Maccabean revolt succeeded. The Greeks lost power. The Hasmonean dynasty regained local control. Actually, the Greeks were not beaten. Instead, the rise of Rome required all their attention, thus that was what they concentrated on, and ignored the Jews. But the Jews saw their withdrawal as an act of God. He was in control after all! The world was not septic after all! Demonology could be discarded.

The second reason, the more important reason, as to why apocalyptic thought was never canonized by the Jews is because the whole doctrine of Satan is naive. It raises more questions than answers. If Satan was so evil, why did God create him in the first place? If God was so mighty, why did he let Satan fall? Why did God tolerate his existence after the fall? Furthermore, an emphasis on Satan shrinks man, denies human responsibility. Thus, Judaism, the parent of Demonology-Eschatology, abandoned it.

Later, as we shall see, the gospel of John did the same. In John, there is no independent enemy. God reigns supreme, man is free, and Eschatology is realized.

But John was later, at the *end* of the New Testament. The opening books of the New Testament, the synoptic gospels, and the letters of Paul are Demonological-Eschatological throughout and entirely. They, like apocalyptic, repudiate the essential thought of the Old Testament, discard the *Principle of Retribution*, and see the world as Satan-controlled.

Ω

## Chapter Four

# Paul: Apocalyptic

············································································

The Old Testament saw God as supreme, the unchallenged ruler of heaven and earth. The *Principle of Retribution* prevailed; if you meditated on the law you would be blessed, be like a tree planted by waters, in all that you did you would prosper. The way of the wicked was not so. The way of the wicked would perish.

That theology was repudiated by apocalyptic, which said that Satan had rebelled, had been cast down to earth, and there he and his horde attacked the Elect, those loyal unto God. But God would act and restore his sovereignty. As God's reign approached, when the world was soon to be cleansed and restored, Satan's wrath would be great because he knew that his time was short.

The double building blocks of apocalyptic were *Demonology* – the conviction that the world was enslaved. And *Eschatology* – the assurance that relief was at hand.

There can be no doubt, Paul swam in that stream. His Demonology is emphatic and non-ambiguous, saturating everything he said. He warns his flock, "Put on the whole armor of God that you may be able to stand against the wiles of the devil. For we are not contending against flesh and blood, but against the principalities, the powers, *against the world rulers* (κοσμοκρατορας) of this present darkness, against the spiritual host of wickedness in the heavenly places...take the whole armor of God that you may be able to...quench the flaming darts of the evil one" (Eph. 6:11-18).

Paul calls Satan "the god of this world" (2 Cor. 4:4). And because Satan is the world ruler, the god of this world, Paul calls the time in which we live "the present *evil* age" (Gal. 1:4).

His Eschatology is equally emphatic and non-ambiguous. In his very first letter, he is so convinced of the imminence of the end that he himself expects to be alive when Jesus returns: "For this I declare to you by the word of the Lord, that *we who are alive,* who are left until the coming of the Lord, shall not precede those who have fallen asleep...And the dead in Christ will rise first, *then we who are alive, who are left,* shall be caught up together with them in the clouds to meet the Lord" (1 Thess. 4:13-17).

It is true, he acknowledges that, though expected soon, the exact hour is unknown to him, and he refers to one of the parables of Jesus, which allowed for a delay: "As to the times and the seasons, brethren, you have no need to have anything written to you. For you yourselves know well that the day of the Lord will come like a thief in the night" (1Thess. 5:1-2).

And it is also true that even the conviction that he personally would be alive when the end arrives, is later set aside. Sitting in prison in Rome, waiting to watch his head roll down the Appian Way, Paul realizes his martyrdom is at hand: "...I am to be poured out as a libation upon the sacrificial offering of your faith..." (Phil. 2:17).

The awareness of his martyrdom preceding the final hour, however, does not diminish the liveliness of the Eschatology expectation. In 1 Cor. 7, his flock asks whether it is all right to marry. His answer is crisp and clear. If you cannot control your passion, if you are in heat all the time and cannot keep your trousers buttoned, then go ahead and marry (1 Cor. 7:9). *But it is better not to.* With the same logic seen in the Essenes of Qumran, he thinks it unwise to bear children and bring them into a Satan-controlled world soon to be thrown into upheaval by the counterattack of the evil one as the final victory draws near: "I think that in view of the present distress it is well for a person to remain as he is...those who marry will have worldly troubles, and I would spare you that. I mean, brethren, the appointed time has grown very short; from now on, let those who have wives live as though they had none" (1 Cor. 7:26-29). The word translated as "present" distress (ενεσωσαν) can also be translated "impending." The end is so close, so impending, that it is already upon us, present.

In Romans, Paul makes clear that the end is not only imminent, in one sense already present. It is also cosmic. It is not an existential internal psychological acknowledgement of the sovereignty of God; it is the literal cleansing of a corrupted creation. "For the creation waits with eager longing...the creation was subjected to futility...the creation itself will be set free from its bondage to decay...the whole creation has been groaning in travail until now" (Rom. 8:19-23). This is the literal physical creation. The word used here is κτισις and its liberation is close. Paul, always graphic in his language, says that the labor pains have already begun!

One of the purposes of the evil one's flaming darts is to attack the Elect and hinder the mission of the church. In 2 Cor. 12:7, Paul attributes his illness, whatever it was, to an activity of Satan because it invaded the effectiveness of his ministry: "a thorn was given me in the flesh, a messenger of Satan, to harass me."

In that same letter, Paul is forced to defend the legitimacy of his apostleship, give evidence of his loyalty to Jesus. And to what does he point? Not to his Sunday school ribbons, not to the trophies on his mantle. He points to his sufferings! "Are they servants of Christ? I am a better one…Five times…the forty lashes…Three times beaten with rods, once I was stoned. Three times I have been shipwrecked…in danger from rivers, in danger from robbers, danger from my own people, danger from Gentiles, danger in the city, danger in the wilderness… in toil and hardship… in hunger and thirst…without food in cold and exposure" (2 Cor. 11:23-27). This is repudiation of Psalm One. It is the apocalyptic rejection of the Old Testament *Principle of Retribution* whereby the good are rewarded.

But always, coupled with the litany of abuse and resistance, there is the unflagging assurance that Christ is stronger and rescue is on the way; there is no need, ever, for despair. This is one of the most impressive of all of the emphases of the Apostle. "For I consider that the sufferings of this present time are not worth comparing with the glory that is to be revealed to us" (Rom. 8:18). "We are afflicted in every way, but not crushed; perplexed, but not driven to despair; persecuted but not forsaken; struck down but not destroyed…knowing that he who raised the Lord Jesus will raise us also… So we do not lose heart" (2 Cor. 4:7-16).

The passage, which carries perhaps the greatest emotional impact, is in Romans chapter 8. The preceding chapter paints the most negative anthropology possible. Just as the demons in the synoptics could invade like a Legion, and hold man helpless, so also Roman 7. Sin for Paul is not a parade of minor *peccadillos*. *Sin is personalized*: "I do not understand my own actions. For I do not do what I want, but I do the very thing I hate…. I can will what is right but I cannot do it…. Now if I do what I do not want, it is no longer I that do it, but sin which dwells within me" (Rom. 7:15-20). *Sin is not an act; it is an enemy holding man in bondage.* Here it has the definite article, η αμαρτια. There is no freedom of the will: "I do not understand my own actions. For I do not do what I want, but I do the very thing I hate...I can will what is right but I cannot do it" (Rom. 7:15-18). We cannot even pray as we ought. The Holy Spirit has to do for us (Rom. 8:26).

But laced throughout the litany of helplessness throbs the hope of rescue: "What then shall we say to these things? If God is for us, who is against us?

Who shall separate us from the love of Christ? Shall tribulation , or distress, or persecution, or famine, or nakedness, or peril, or sword?...No, in all these things we are more than conquerors...For I am sure that neither death, nor life, nor angels, nor principalities, nor things present, nor things to come, nor powers, nor height, nor depth, nor anything else in all creation will be able to separate us from the love of God in Christ Jesus our Lord" (Rom. 8:31-39).

This unwavering confidence that Christ will deliver from the wrath, which is to come, is omnipresent. In his first letter, 1 Thess. 1:10. Jesus is called τον ρυομενον, *The Deliverer*, who will shield us from the wrath about to erupt as the end approaches and the evil one counterattacks. And in one of the pastorals, so late it is perhaps posthumous, we read "I know whom I have believed, and I am sure that he is able to guard until that Day what has been entrusted to me" (2 Tim. 1:12).

The weapons used by the angels, principalities, and powers to afflict the elect seeking to separate them from the love of God are all the scourges listed in apocalyptic: famine, nakedness, peril, sword. Prominent among them is death. Death is not a sweet release of a heavenly Father gently calling his children homeward, nor is it a divine punishment stemming from God. *Death is an enemy,* the final or greatest enemy, Satan's most powerful weapon. "The last enemy to be destroyed is death" (1 Cor. 15:26).

First Corinthians 2:8 is a difficult passage, so terse that one cannot emphatically insist that any interpretation offered up is correct: "None of the rulers of this age understood this; for if they had, they would not have crucified the Lord of glory."

The rulers of this age are not Pilate and Caiaphas. Elsewhere Paul insisted that the κοσμοκρατορας of this present evil age were the principalities and powers, the spiritual host of wickedness in the heavenly places. Their strongest weapon was death. They thought they could stem the relentless advance of the rule of God and retain control of their stolen realm by crucifying Jesus.

They overestimated their strength. Their attempt to end the relentless advance of the kingdom of God failed. Christ was stronger! Hence the thunderous exclamation of Paul that the resurrection was the irrefutable historical evidence that liberation of the cosmos was assured: "Now if Christ is preached as raised from the dead, how can some of you say that there is no resurrection of the dead"…if Christ has not been raised, then our preaching is in vain, and your faith is in vain…If Christ has not been raised, your faith is futile and you are still in your sins…If for this life only we have hoped in Christ, we are of all men most to be pitied. But in fact Christ has been raised from the dead…so also in Christ shall all be made alive. But each in his own order: Christ the first fruits, then at his coming those who belong to Christ. Then, comes the end, when he delivers the kingdom to God the Father after destroying every rule and power…The last enemy to be destroyed is death… 'Death is swallowed up in victory. O, death, where is thy victory? O, death, where is thy sting?'… thanks be to God, who gives the victory through our Lord Jesus Christ" (1 Cor. 15:12-27, 54-57).

Ω

## CHAPTER FIVE

# THE SYNOPTICS: APOCALYPTIC

A century ago it was easily said, Paul was not an apostle, he was a perverter. In France, Ernst Renan called him "an ugly little Jew." With a start like that, it had to get worse. Renan went on to say, "The writings of Paul have been a peril and a stumbling block, the cause of the principle defects of Christian theology."[1]

Across the channel in England, David Lindsay said the same thing in doggerel: "By him that bore the crown of thorn, I would St. Paul had never been born."[2]

And in Germany as well. Lindsay said it in sixteen words. Because he was German, it took Adolph Von Harnack four volumes to say the same thing. But it *was* the same thing. He

---

1. Archibald Macbride Hunter, *Interpreting Paul's Gospel* (Philadelphia: Westminster Press, 1955), 13.

2. Ibid.

asked "What Is Christianity?" and the answer was, it began one way, horizontal, an ethical exhortation of Jesus, and ended up another way, vertical, fabricated by Paul into a colossal cosmic scheme of salvation.

Now that Demonology and Eschatology are recognized as base of Jesus' message (pages 8-9 above) such indictments are no longer possible. Paul was no perverter. Jesus and Paul share the same world view, stand shoulder to shoulder.

\*\*\*

In Luke chapter 13, Jesus repudiates the Principle of Retribution: "Do you think that these Galileans were worse sinners than all the other Galileans because they suffered thus? I tell you, No!" (Luke 13:2). He repudiates it a second time: "Or those eighteen upon whom the tower in Siloam fell and killed them, do you think that they were worse sinners than all the others who dwelt in Jerusalem? I tell you, No!" (Luke 13:4) Having rejected the Old Testament Principle, he then sides with the apocalyptic conviction that suffering came from Satan and was an attack on the Elect: "Ought not this woman, *a daughter of Abraham whom Satan bound* for eighteen years, be loosed from her bond on the Sabbath day?" (Luke 13:16).

His identification with apocalyptic thought is most clearly seen in his miracles. In the oldest record of the life of Jesus, there is no sermon, neither plain nor mount, and few parables. Instead, Mark is about 80 percent miracle.

Statistically the number one miracle is exorcism. It is also his first miracle. In the Capernaum synagogue, an unclean spirit has invaded a man, holds him helpless, and takes control of his vocal chords: "What have you to do with us, Jesus of Nazareth? Have you come to destroy us? I know who you are, the Holy One of God. But Jesus rebuked him saying, 'Be silent and come out of him!'" (Mark 1:25).

The word επετιμησεν is better translated not "rebuked" but "attacked." And the basic meaning of φιμωθητι is to make still, to throttle or strangle. The demon asks, "Have you come to destroy us?" And Jesus attacks and strangles!

Exorcisms are not only numerically superior, they are also theologically the most significant. The works and the words of Jesus are welded into one, they are a unity. With his words he says the kingdom of God is coming. And in exorcisms it actually comes. When a demon is attacked and throttled, a beach head has been established, an area where Satan no longer rules. Where a demon is routed, the rule of God is restored: "But if it is by the finger of God that I cast out demons, then the kingdom of God has come upon you" (Luke 11:20).

Exorcisms are *direct* attacks on the person of the demons. The other miracles are *indirect* attacks. They undo the damage the demons have done. The demons cause hunger. Jesus feeds the multitude and there are baskets of bread left over. Eventually, soon, when the cosmic battle is finally ended, hunger will be entirely overcome. The elect will come from east and west to banquet with Abraham and Isaac and Jacob (Luke 13:29). The feeding of the five thousand is a foretaste of the heavenly feast to come. Since hunger is not the will of God, the only negative miracle Jesus works on land is to curse the barren fig tree (Matt. 21:19).

The demons also cause illness, thus Jesus heals the sick, makes the lame to walk, and opens blind eyes. Peter's mother-in-law is ill, so he "rebukes" the fever just as he rebuked the evil spirit, and immediately she is restored to health, "saved." Σωσω literally means to be restored to health.

And the demons do damage to nature itself. The savagery of the sea is sweeping away his disciples! So Jesus "rebuked the wind, and said to the sea, 'Peace, be still!' And the wind ceased, and there was a great calm" (Mark 4:39). The same words are used on the demoniac in Capernaum, facing the fever, and stilling of the storm because the enemy is always the same. Since there is a lethal unity to the evil empire, there is a unity in the miracles of Jesus. They hang together. If you understand one, you understand them all (Mark 6:51-52).

These attacks arouse resistance. *Counterattack* is a constant. In Matt. 13:24-30, Jesus speaks of an enemy perverting the harvest by sowing weeds. The demons striking back is the thought of Luke 11:24-26 as well: "When the unclean spirit has gone out of a man, he passes through waterless places seeking rest, and finding none he says 'I will return to the house from which I came,'...then he goes and brings seven other spirits more evil than himself, and they enter and dwell there; and the last state of that man becomes worse than the first."

The counterattack began when the Baptist first announced that the kingdom of God was at hand: "From the days of John the Baptist until now the kingdom of heaven has suffered violence, and men of violence take it by force" (Matt. 11:12). βιασται does not refer to "*men* of violence" but to "the violent ones," demonic forces, who resist the restoration of God's rule. They succeeded in their counterattack against the Baptist. He was the forerunner of Jesus in more ways than one. He was executed.

Counterattack is the key to the Messianic secret, Jesus' demand for silence after a mighty work. After healing the leper, "he sternly charged him...'See that you say nothing to any one'" (Mark 1:43). After raising Jairus' daughter, "he strictly charged them that no one should know this:" (Mark 5:43). He makes a deaf man to hear, "And he charged them to tell no one" (Mark 7:36).

The healed person is visible evidence of the superiority of Jesus. Thus, that person is in great danger! The demons will seek to retake the lost ground! Be silent, lest the evil spirit come back with seven more lethal than itself!

The Lord's Prayer is apocalyptic throughout, and protection from the counterattack is central. First, Jesus requests that just as Satan was defeated on high and thrown to earth, so also may he be subdued down here as well: "Thy kingdom come, thy will be done on earth as it is in heaven."

But Satan will fight back, to hold onto his plundered posses-sion. And one of the weapons he will use is hunger. Sustenance will be needed if one is to survive! Jesus earlier indicated that when the final victory is won, there will be bread in abundance. The elect will come from east and west to eat with Abraham (Matt. 8:11). The popular present translations are an exegetical tap dance, not even coming close to what the text actually says. Jesus does not say "Give us this day our daily bread," as if there is a fore-ordained allotment of biscuits available each day. What the Greek literally says is "Give us some of that *future* bread now!" When the victory is finally won, hunger abolished, there will be bread in abundance. Since we have called for the kingdom to come, counterattack will include hunger. We need sustenance *now*! Sustain us now, in the throes of this final struggle, with some of that banquet bread!

But hunger is not the only weapon, which will be used as the kingdom comes closer, nor is it even the major weapon. There will be a time of trouble, a scale of savage fury never before seen (Mark 13:19)!

Πειρασμος has two meanings. One is psychological, and the translation is "temptation." The other meaning is objective and describes a brutal bludgeoning. That is the way the word is used in The Lord's Prayer. Again, timid translators have emptied out the meaning of what Jesus is actually saying, for fear of giving credence to language, which makes the *modern sophisticate* uncomfortable. Jesus does *not* say, "lead us not into temptation."

What he does say is the plea, "See to it Lord, we are spared from the savage brutal bludgeoning about to be launched by the "evil one." Not "evil" in general. The definite article is there, τον πονερον!

It is disgraceful, sinful, cowardly, a disservice to serious

Bible study, to water down and weaken what Jesus says simply because an effete cosmopolitan finds such archaic language distasteful. Why bother to preserve and memorize the Prayer if we disdain what it actually says? Here, as everywhere else in the synoptic gospels, Jesus' message is apocalyptic, grounded in demonology and eschatology, despite the tremors and spasms of intimidated translators. What is actually said is, "Heavenly Father, just as you cleansed the pent house and threw Satan out, now do the same down here! We know there will be furious resistance, so give an advance installment of the heavenly feast to sustain us. And see to it that we are not exposed to the full brunt of Satan's final resistance. The final line, "Lead us not into temptation, but deliver us from evil," if rightly translated, would read: "Lead us not into the final attack of the evil one, but deliver us from him."

Consternation over the catastrophic coming counterattack is what prompted Jesus' remark in Luke. Just as the Essenes had foregone sexual activity, refusing to bring children into an enslaved world subject to the woes of the evil one (page 27 above), just as Paul urged that those who had wives to live as though they had none because the present form of the world was passing away (page 31 above), so also Jesus grieves over those who are pregnant in that final hour: "Alas for those who are with child and for those who give suck in those days. For great distress shall be upon the earth, and wrath upon this people" (Luke 21:23).

*\*\*\**

Jesus did not accommodate himself to the views of those around him. He did not endorse the demons merely to gain entrée unto his audience. Jesus always had a *higher* regard for the savage strength of Satan than did his contemporaries. He is accused of being "possessed by Beelzebul, and by the prince of demons he cast out the demons" (Mark 3:22). His critics see the demons as disorganized, engaged in petty intramural warfare, one casting out another. Jesus sees them as a lethal unit. "How can Satan cast out Satan?...if Satan has risen up against himself and is divided, he cannot stand" (Mark 3:23-26).

Jesus' view of Satan was already higher than that of those around him, and as his ministry unrolled, he was forced to elevate that view ever upwards. He began with a strong view of Satan, and ended up with an even stronger awareness of the evil one's strength.

That is the drama of Matthew chapter ten. Jesus' ministry had been successful thus far. He was convinced Satan's empire would soon topple.

Hunger had been overcome, storms stilled, dead raised, demons cast out, so many beach heads established that it appeared that one enormous final push would make the weakened Satan kingdom collapse like a house of cards. If the attack on Satan were expanded, if the number of those casting out demons and healing the sick were raised – no longer by him alone but by his disciples as well – the end would come quickly.

In Matthew 10:2-4 there is a roll call. Those who are to carry out the final push are solemnly named. Matthew 10:1 they are deputized, the powers of Jesus are delegated to them: "He gave to them authority over unclean spirits, to cast them out, and to heal every disease and infirmity."

Because there will soon be twelve of them attacking the Satanic realm, the end will come quickly. The blitzkrieg (lightning war) will prove so effective that they will not have to go far! The itinerary is sharply limited. No need to go to the Decapolis nor into Samaria. Limit themselves to the "house of Israel" (Matt. 10:5-6). All they had to do and say was what Jesus had done and said: "And preach as you go, saying, 'The kingdom of heaven is at hand.' Heal the sick, raise the dead, cleanse lepers, cast out demons" (Matt. 10:7-8).

That will be enough! Even though the itinerary is limited, they won't even have time to cover even that sparse an area! "I say to you, you will not have gone through all the towns of Israel, before the Son of man comes" (Matt. 10:23).

The Son of man was to come in glory, yet not one word has been said so far about his death! *Their* efforts would be enough!

But their efforts were *not* enough. They returned. The blitzkrieg failed to achieve the predicted result. Jesus must rethink the situation. He abruptly withdraws. The Galilean spring time ends. He retreats to Caesarea Philippi. His ministry has to be rethought, reconstructed. Satan was stronger than earlier recognized. New procedures had to be drawn up and put into place.

It is at Caesarea Philippi that Jesus at last recognizes that only he, not the disciples, can overcome the evil one. Jesus personally must enter into and overcome Satan's most powerful weapon, death. It is at Caesarea Philippi that the *very first* announcement of Jesus' death is made: "And Jesus went on with his disciples to the villages of Caesarea Philippi…And *he began* to teach them that the Son of man must suffer many things, and be rejected by the elders and the chief priests and the scribes, and be killed. And after three days, rise again. And he said this plainly" (Mark 8:27,31-32). That this is indeed the very first time the death of Jesus has ever been aired is verified by the reaction of Peter. Peter is stupefied. He emphatically rejects what Jesus just said (Mark 8:32).

That is not the first time that Satan has shown himself to be stronger than he was understood to be. It had happened before, at the baptism of Jesus.

Already then, early on at the outset, at his baptism, Jesus had been obliged to elevate upward his evaluation of Satan. The baptism of John was supposed to be a protective overcoat shielding the baptized from Satan's counterattack. Because his rite was such a shield was why the Baptist refused to baptize those whom he held unworthy of such protection: "But when he saw many of the Pharisees and Sadducees coming for baptism, he said to them, 'You brood of vipers! Who warned you to flee from the wrath to come?'" (Matt. 3:7).

Jesus having been baptized should have been shielded from Satanic attack. But he wasn't. Satan pierced through shielding overcoat. Jesus was attacked and tempted, πειρασμος.

There is a sequence to the scene at the Jordan. Jesus is identified by the voice from heaven as the Son of God: "This is my beloved Son, with whom I am well pleased" (Matt. 3:17). And Satan seeks to sow seeds of doubt, undermine that identification. God cannot go hungry. God opens his hand and feeds every living thing. "*If you are* the Son of God"(Matt. 4:3) why are you hungry? Turn these stones into bread and eat. Prove to yourself that what you just heard from on high is so! "*If you are* the Son of God, (Matt. 4:6) prove it by throwing yourself down from the temple top. God cannot be hurt!"

Jesus warded off those doubts by ordering Satan away: "Begone, Satan!" (Matt.4:16). Luke adds that "when the devil had ended every temptation, he departed from him until an opportune time" (Luke 4:13).

Caesarea Philippi was that more opportune time. The sequence of the scene at the Jordan unrolls anew at Caesarea Philippi. The perplexity of Peter is shared by Jesus. Jesus is attacked, tempted, a second time. The Jordan ordeal is repeated. *If he is* the Son of God, how can he die? God cannot die. He wards off this doubt as he did the earlier one with the same words to Peter that were uttered at the Jordan, "Get behind me, Satan!" (Mark 8:33).

Once the blitzkrieg failed, Jesus had to retreat and reformulate his plan of attack. The disciples could not do it. Jesus himself had to do it. His ministry must start all over again. The two events that marked the original beginning of his ministry were twofold: the voice from heaven and the temptation. They

**43**

both are repeated at Caesarea because the ministry begins all over again. The voice from heaven speaks in Mark 9:17 as it had in Matt.9:17. Satan is rebuffed in Mark 9:17 with exactly the same words uttered earlier in Matt. 4:16

He now knows what must be done. He will enter into death and overcome it, and this will accomplish what the disciples were unable to achieve. Once his resurrection has taken place, Satan's fall will follow quickly. Thus, the prediction of his death and resurrection (Mark 8:31-32) are followed almost immediately by him telling the disciples that the end will come in their lifetime: "Truly, I say to you there are some standing here who will not taste death before they see that the kingdom of God has come with power" (Mark 9:1).

With that he sets out for Jerusalem in such haste that the disciples are astounded: "And they were on the road, going up to Jerusalem, and Jesus was walking ahead of them, and they were amazed" (Mark 10:32).

His personal attack on Satan's strongest weapon, death, will precipitate Satan's strongest counterattack. The Little Apocalypse is where the awesome dimensions of Satan's final resistance to the restoration of God's rule are most graphically described: "...wars and rumors of wars...nation will rise against nation...this is but the beginning of the birth-pangs... brother will deliver up brother to death, and the father his child...you will be hated by all...in those days there will be such tribulation as has not been from the beginning of the creation until now...in those days the sun will be darkened, and the moon will not give its light, and the stars will be falling from heaven, and the powers in the heaven will be shaken" (Mark 13:7,12,19,24-25). The enemy is finally overcome, at last the Son of man can come and gather the elect (Mark 13:26).

True, he acknowledges that of "that day or that hour, no one knows, not even the angels in heaven, nor the Son of man, but only the Father" (Mark 13:32), to which he added, "Watch therefore – for you do not know when the master of the house will come, in the evening or at midnight, or at cockcrow, or in the morning…I say to you, Watch" (Mark 13:35-37).

To that caution, he had earlier added the parable of the foolish maidens who were surprised by the bridegroom's delay and failed to put oil in their lamps (Matt. 25:1-13). And he spoke of the end coming at a time unknown, like a thief in the night (Matt. 24:42-44). But it is clear that in the heat of expectancy these cautionary asides received little or no immediate attention as Jesus hurries to Jerusalem.

\* \* \*

Jesus was hurrying to Jerusalem not to preach but to die. That weak-kneed band of jelly-legged commentators who bleat that Jesus went to Jerusalem to preach, and his death was unexpected, his prediction of Caesarea Philippi dismissed as *vaticinia ex eventu*,[3] ought be ashamed. There is nothing in the way the march to Jerusalem is presented to justify such a distortion.

His reputation had preceded him. Knowing that he could walk on water, had stilled storms and multiplied bread and raised the dead, the people were convinced he could cast out Rome as well. His arrival precipitated a tumultuous welcome, branches of palms cast before him, robes in the road. He had to alter the mood – turn adulation into anger — if he was to realize his reason for coming to Jerusalem. This he did by cleansing the temple the very next day and castigating the authorities for having defiled the temple with pigeon sales and feigned piety!

Aroused, the authorities decided to proceed against him as they had earlier intended (Mark 3:6). But they had decided to delay due to the passions of Passover (Mark 14:1-2). Judas' unexpected offer to lead them to a place where Jesus could be

---

3. See Footnote 3, ii.

arrested in the middle of the night, thus not arousing a tumult among the people, changed their minds.

Jesus was seized and hustled off to a quick kangaroo court. Because it was last minute, no time for preparation, they were unable to consolidate the testimonies of hired witnesses. When those false testimonies broke down (Mark 14:59), the high priest resorted to desperation tactics and sought to get the accused to testify against himself, an illegal tactic (Mark 14:60-61).

Jesus was asked whether he was the Christ. It was a political term. To be the Christ, or Messiah, was to be the anointed one, the king. Though the term Christ was devoid of religious overtones and was purely political, a confession would have been enough to turn him over to the Romans as guilty of sedition, a political revolutionary.

The trial would have end had Jesus remained silent! They had no other evidence against him! But Jesus had come to die, so when they asked if he were the Christ, he gave them the evidence they needed. He gave them more than they expected! He concedes that he is the Christ, making him guilty of hostility toward Rome, but he goes further than that! He uses the terminology of the Dead Sea people and calls himself the Son of Man, the divine redeemer who will lead the sons of light and overpower the sons of darkness (page 27 above): "I am, and you will see the Son of man seated at the right hand of Power, and coming with the clouds of heaven" (Mark 14:62).

Politics is no longer the issue! Religion is! Jesus has just committed blasphemy! "Why do we still need witnesses? You have heard his blasphemy. What is your decision? And they all condemned him as deserving death" (Mark 14:63-64).

So it was that Jesus brought about what he predicted at Caesarea Philippi. He was never a victim. He was always in control. Maudlin sympathy is rejected: "…do not weep for me, but weep for yourselves" (Luke 23:28). He staggers and falls under the crushing weight of wood and insult, but picks up his cross and goes to Golgotha with a show of such strength that the Roman officer in charge exclaims, "Truly this man was the Son of God" (Mark 15:39). Not a confession of Christian faith, but an awed admiration, that Jesus was not helpless and abused, but was in control.

Executed and then raised, death being unable to hold Him, Jesus ascends to the Father: "…he was lifted up and a cloud took him out of their sight. And while they were gazing into heaven as he went, behold, two men stood by them in white robes, and said, 'Men of Galilee, why do you stand looking into heaven? This Jesus, who was taken up from you into heaven, will come in the same way as you saw him go into heaven" (Acts 1:10-11).

The cautionary notes that the end might be delayed were at first never taken seriously, the hope of an immediate end was too high and heated. Thus, the synoptic narrative ends with the disciples standing on tip toe, awaiting the promised return.

Ω

# CHAPTER SIX

# JOHN: APOCALYPTIC REPUDIATED

The gospel of John tells us that Jesus never did predict that the end would come during the lifetime of the disciples! That was a misunderstanding! "When Peter saw him, he said to Jesus, 'Lord what about this man?' Jesus said to him, 'If it is my will that he remain until I come, what is that to you? Follow me!' The saying spread abroad among the brethren that his disciple was not to die; yet Jesus did not say to him that he was not to die, but 'if it is my will that he remain until I come, what is that to you?'" (John 21:21-23).

There was no need to look for the return of Jesus because he had already returned! In the garden, after the resurrection, he told Mary not to touch him because he had not yet ascended to the Father: "Jesus said to her, 'Do not hold me, for I have not yet ascended to my Father" (John 20:17).

Yet only eight days later he *can* be touched! He not only has ascended, he has returned! Thus, he can say to Thomas, "Put

your finger here, and see my hands, and put out your hand
and place it in my side" (John 20:27).

There is no need to look for the return of Jesus to reestablish
the rule of God. God is *already* in control! So-called "enemies"
have no independent power.

They are already servants, subdued, performing only the will
of God who is absolute and in total control. They may be unknowing servants, ignorant of the fact that they are controlled
by God, but unknowing or not, what they do is not their will
but God's. *Old Testament thought returns!* Just as Assyria was
summoned by God and was his servant (page 15 above), so
also Caiaphas was a servant. He, a supposed enemy, about to
execute Jesus, succinctly summarizes the entire redemptive
ministry of Jesus: "You do not understand that it is expedient
for you, that one man should die for the people, and that the
whole nation should not perish" (John 11:50). This was no
mere coincidence of language that one supposedly hostile
and independent should say so penetratingly why Jesus had
come and would die. Caiaphas was only a servant: "He did not
say this of his own accord, but being high priest that year he
prophesied that Jesus should die for the nation" (John 11:51).

God alone is in charge. It is Isaiah all over again (pages
15-16 above). Pilate seeks to cow Jesus into submission by
boasting of his power over him (John 19:10), to which comes
the deflating description that Pilate is but a puppet, a pawn in
God's hand, devoid of any personal authority or significance:
"You would have no power over me, unless it had been given
you from above" (John 19:11).

In the same way, Judas, the arch enemy and ultimate be-
trayer, does not move a muscle until ordered to do so by Jesus
himself: "What you are going to do, do quickly" (John 13:27).

Because God and God alone is the actor, suffering is no
longer attributable to Satan as an attack on the elect. The Old
Testament *Principle of Retribution* is restored. If you sin, divine

punishment follows. Thus, Jesus, after healing a man who had been ill for thirty-eight years cautions him, "See, you are well! Sin no more that nothing worse befall you" (John 5:14).

There is no Demonology in the Old Testament (page 18 above). Nor is there any in John. The statistical number one miracle in the synoptics, exorcism, is erased, gone entirely. In John, to be under the power of the devil is not due to invasion by an irresistible foe like unto a legion, able to seize your vocal cords. Instead, it is the consequence of existential decision. One has stopped up one's ears and spurns Jesus' words: "Why do you not understand what I say? It is because you cannot bear to hear my word. You are of your father the devil" (John 8:43-44).

The need is not for evil spirits to be rebuked and stilled (attacked and throttled). Release will come when the responsible one repents and embraces Jesus in faith. Salvation is not a future event when sheep and goats are separated. It is *now*, in the present hour, when one believes: "He who believes in him is not condemned; he who does not believe is condemned *already* because he has not believed" (John 3:19).

Satan's usurped authority is not to be ended in a climactic final hour of Eschatology. It ended already, at the cross. The gospel of John gives no detailing of precisely *how* Satan's sovereignty was shorn and *how* he was subdued and subjected to servanthood anew. But while there are no details as to how it took place, *it has already* taken place.

Three times Satan is referred to in apocalyptic terms. And each time, his impotence is underlined. His subjugation is not future, it is then, that hour, during the ministry of Jesus: "*Now* is the judgment of this world, *now* shall the ruler of this world be cast out" (John 12:31). "I will no longer talk much with you, for the ruler of this world is coming. *He has no power over me*" (John 14:30). Again, "…the ruler of this world *is* judged" (John 16:11).

The emphasis is shifted backwards to the cross. In the synoptics and in Paul, the resurrection was the vital beating heart of the proclamation because it was the turning point, historical proof that the most powerful weapon of Satan, death, was unable to hold Jesus, thus eventual victory was guaranteed at his return. In John, however, the critical moment is not future, neither *parousia* nor resurrection. God's sovereignty was fully restored at the cross. Only in John can Jesus say from the cross, "It is finished" (John 19:30).

It is only an artist, not a theologian, who recognized this. Salvatore Dali painted the cross as a soaring triumph dwarfing all below and entitled it. "The Christ of St. John of the Cross."

Satan was not a name but a legal term meaning adversary or prosecutor (page 18 above). In every court room, there are *two* lawyers. The prosecutor or adversary indicting. And the defense attorney, the Counselor, a friend, defending.

In the very contexts where John insists that Satan is shorn of power, the promise is made that the adversary will be replaced by the counselor. The new legal representative on high will no longer be a threat, Satan, but a friend, the Holy Spirit: "And I will pray the Father, and he will give you another Counselor, to be with you for ever…I will not leave you desolate" (John 14:16-18). "But the Counselor, the Holy Spirit, whom the Father will send in my name, he will teach you all things… Peace I leave with you" (John 14:25-27). "But when the Counselor comes, whom I shall send to you…the Spirit of truth…because you have been with me from the beginning" (John 15:26). The Holy Spirit replaces Satan as the legal agent from on high. Old Testament theology has been reaffirmed. God rules through his angelic host, but now that angelic host is affirmative and protective, not suspicious and hostile, and seeks to comfort, not indict.

The *Principle of Retribution* has been affirmed. Suffering comes from God. But there is one fundamental difference.

No longer is its purpose purely punitive!. Suffering can have a positive purpose. That positive purpose may not be immediately visible, but it is there nonetheless.

In John 9:1 the disciples ask Jesus, "Rabbi, who sinned, this man or his parents, that he was born blind?" Jesus does not deny their assumption that God was the source of the affliction, but he does insist there was a purpose to it. "It was not that this man sinned, or his parents, but that the works of God might be made manifest in him" (John 9:3). The purpose was that when the man was given sight, Jesus could be seen as the light of the world! Jesus might be seen as of God: "Never since the world began has it been heard that any one opened the eyes of a man born blind. If this man were not from God, he could do nothing" (John 9:32).

Three times are we told that Jesus loved Lazarus (John 11:3,5,36). What should one do when told that a loved one is dying? Rush to him of course! But what does Jesus do? "So when he heard that he was ill, he stayed two days longer in the place where he was" (John 11:6). Jesus *deliberately* tarried! He *waited* for Lazarus to die, and was *glad* when it happened! "Then Jesus told them plainly, 'Lazarus is dead, and for your sake I am glad I was not there, so that you may believe" (John 11:14). The death of Lazarus had a purpose. "This illness is not unto death; it is for the glory of God, so that the Son of God may be glorified by means of it" (John 11:5).

It was not punishment but revelatory. It made it possible for Jesus to say and for them to believe that "I am the resurrection and the life; he who believes in me though he die, yet shall he live, and whoever lives and believes in me shall never die. Do you believe this?" (John 11:25-26). The purpose of that suffering, unseen at the outset, was to enable one to believe!

Since Demonology has been denied and man is recognized as responsible, called to account and able to believe, the purpose of the death in John is different in John. In the synoptics, it was the doorway to victory, only a means, access unto the resurrection, the road that led to the *parousia*. In John, it is an end in itself. It achieves something in its own right. It covers man's guilt. It serves the same purpose as the Lamb of God in the Old Testament.

In the Old Testament, a little lamb was a vicarious replacement for human guilt. The transgressions of the individual were placed on the head of the little lamb, and when slain, the offerer was cleansed, freed of guilt. John abandons the *Christus Victor*[4] motif, that Jesus had come to destroy the devil and all his works, and returns to Old Testament themes: "Surely he has borne our griefs, and carried our sorrows...he was smitten by God and afflicted...wounded for our transgressions, he was bruised for our iniquities, upon him was the chastisement that made us whole...the Lord has laid on him the iniquity of us all" (Isaiah 53:4-6).

Because this is the theology of John, he must alter the day of the crucifixion. He must make the cross, not the resurrection, central. Jesus must die not after the Passover meal has already been eaten as in the synoptics. He must die on the day of preparation for the Passover, at the very moment that the lamb of God is slain. "Then they led Jesus from the house of Caiaphas to the praetorium. It was early. They themselves did not enter the praetorium, so that they might not be defiled, but might eat the Passover" (John 18:28). It had to happen that way to validate the Old Testament: "For these things took place that the scripture might be fulfilled" (John 19:36).

He was dying not as τον ρυομενον, *The Deliverer*, liberating men from sin as bondage after the resurrection at the *parousia*, He was dying as the suffering servant, the lamb of God, paying the price of man's guilt on the cross. That was the way the Baptist identified him in the very first chapter: "The

---

4. The term *Christus Victor* refers to a Christian understanding of the atonement, which views Christ's death as the means by which the powers of evil, which held humankind under their dominion, were defeated.

next day he saw Jesus coming toward him, and said, 'Behold the Lamb of God, who takes away the sin of the world!...The next day again John was standing with two of his disciples; and he looked at Jesus as he walked and said 'Behold the Lamb of God'" (John 1:29, 35-37).

Ω

## CHAPTER SEVEN

# THE NEW TESTAMENT AT ODDS WITH ITSELF

The persecutions by Epiphanes had forced a radical reexamination and consequent rejection of Old Testament theology and its replacement by apocalyptic thought. Paul and the synoptics are built upon apocalyptic thought with its two foci, Demonology and Eschatology.

However, just as Epiphanes forced a radical reexamination and rejection of Old Testament thought, in the same way the collapse of Eschatology forced a radical reexamination and rejection of apocalyptic thought. That is what the Apostle John did. He rejected Demonology and Eschatology and returned to Old Testament convictions.

As a consequence, the two ends of the New Testament are polar opposites.

The early half, Paul and the synoptics, insist that the world is enslaved under Satan. But John insists that God is the sole actor. It is God's will, which is already being done on earth as it is in heaven. The so-called enemies of Jesus — Caiaphas, Pilate, and Judas — are God's servants controlled by God.

For Paul and the synoptics, sin is bondage, a legion of evil able to invade and hold man helpless so that he beats himself with chains and has to cry out "I can will what is right but I cannot do it." John insists that man is free and sin is unbelief. The refusal to hear the words of Jesus is what makes one a child of the devil: the phrase is meant existentially, not metaphysically.

The early books of the New Testament insist that suffering originates in the enemy Satan and is aimed primarily at the elect. John returns to the Old Testament view that suffering stems from God. It is not necessarily always punitive. Ordinarily it has a positive purpose, even if that purpose is not immediately known.

For Paul and the synoptics, Jesus dies to destroy the devil and all his works and all his ways. The cross is but a doorway to the resurrection, which assures victory at the *parousia*. But for John, Jesus is the lamb of God who expiates man's guilt. This work is completed at the cross: "it is finished."

The list of opposites can be extended ad infinitum because every single area of significant theology is affected by the fact that Demonology and Eschatology dominate the early books but are denied in the later books. The long overdue recognition of Demonology and Eschatology in the synoptic gospels is what has forced upon contemporary Christian scholarship the realization that the two ends of the New Testament are at odds with another, that they are polar opposites.

It is not just the fourth gospel, which rebuffs apocalyptic. John does it most thoroughly, but other books say the same thing. Hebrews does not see the world rulers as a spiritual host of wickedness in the heavenly places. Instead, the heavenly host is portrayed positively as "ministering spirits sent forth to serve" (Heb. 1:14). Suffering is not seen as Satan afflicting the elect, but rather as the loving chastisement of God, disciplining his children: "My son, do not regard lightly the discipline of the

Lord, nor lose courage when you are punished by him. For the Lord disciplines him whom he loves, and chastises every son whom he receives. It is for discipline that you have to endure. God is treating you as sons, for what son is there whom his father does not discipline? If you are left without discipline… you are illegitimate children" (Heb. 12:5-8).

It is true that in Hebrews some of the earlier language of apocalyptic remains: "Since therefore the children share in flesh and blood, he himself partook of the same nature, that through death he might destroy him who has the power of death, that is the devil" (Heb.2:14). But while the language lingers on, the emphasis has already passed from the *Christus Victor* motif to a Penitential grasp of the atonement. The terminology, chapter after chapter, of Jesus as high priest (Heb.4:15), learning obedience as he suffered (Heb. 5:7-9), comparing him to Melchizedek (Heb.5:6), and going on to insist that "he holds his priesthood permanently" indicate that now Old Testament thought, not apocalyptic, is to the fore.

The same can be said of John's other writings. 1 John 5:19, like Hebrews 2:14 is merely a remnant of earlier language emptied of content. Revelation is not apocalyptic because in apocalyptic, suffering is an attack by Satan.

True, Rev. 12:7-12 says "the devil has come down to you in great wrath because he knows that his time is short." In the gospel of John supposed enemies are actually servants of God executing God's will (Caiaphas said this not of his own accord, but as priest he was prophesying [page 50 above]). So also here in Revelation. Satan has been tethered. Unknowingly, unwillingly, he is but a servant. Revelation insists repeatedly, in almost every chapter, that the final wrath is purgative punishment coming from God. Satan is merely an agent.

The people on the mainland are suffering because of the persecutions of Domitian, and have come to the conclusion that God has abandoned them. John, from Patmos, reverses it in each of the opening letters to the seven churches, making it clear that it is not God who has abandoned them but they who have abandoned God! The pattern to the seven letters is unmistakable. First, a word of praise: "I know your works, your toil and your patient endurance, and how you cannot bear evil men" (Rev. 2:2). But then comes the indictment: "But I have this against you, that you have abandoned the love you had at first:" (Rev. 2:4). The seventh letter is scathing: "So, because you are lukewarm, and neither cold nor hot, I will spew you out of my mouth" (Rev. 3:16).

Revelation 3:18 is the key and the core of Revelation. Because they have abandoned the love they had at first, because they are now lukewarm, they must be chastised. "Those whom I love I reprove and chasten, so be zealous and repent."

They must be chastened. Every woe poured out in Revelation is not the work of an enemy afflicting them but of God cleansing them. God rules the world, Demonology is denied: "Holy, holy, holy is the Lord God Almighty, who was and is and is to come" (Rev. 4:8). And it is from Almighty God, eternal and in control, that the woes unroll. In chapter 6, it is the Lamb himself who opens the seal and sends out the four horsemen. In Rev. 8:1, in Rev. 9:1, in Rev. 10:1, again and again it is always an angel in heaven who unleashes pain, because those whom God loves he chastens. Never in Revelation is there any doubt that the wrath searing the earth originates in God himself. Rev. 6:16, 14:10, 14:19, 15:1, 15:7, 16:1, 16:19, and 19:15 label their suffering as "the wrath of God." When he has finished his cleansing, Satan can be discarded.

* * *

The two ends of the New Testament cannot be reconciled. They say two different things in every significant area. Is the New Testament to be abandoned because its basic parts are inconsistent one with the other?

Ω

## CHAPTER EIGHT

# DIALECTICAL THOUGHT: VERB VERSUS NOUN

The Hebrew language is built on the verb. The basic building block of Hebrew thought is the three consonant verb. All parts of speech and all emphases of thought grow out of that. Because the Hebrew thought in terms of verbs, his emphasis was not on essence but action. Act or deed, not substance, is where the stress lay.

The basic building block of Greek, however, was the noun. The Greek thought in terms of essence, substance. That was primary, not act.

A Greek could not have written Genesis 1:1. Only a Hebrew could do that: "In the beginning God created heaven and earth." God is in action, doing. The Greek would have had to begin by defining God, his essence, what he is, substance, and only then proceed unto what he did.

The difference between Hebrew and Greek thought is reflected in the earliest creeds. The Apostles Creed was not, of course, created by the Apostles, but the title is apt because it reflects Hebrew thought. The divinity of Jesus is confessed with verbs, not nouns. "Conceived of the Holy Ghost…born of the Virgin Mary." And his humanity is expressed in verbs, not nouns. "Suffered under Pontius Pilate, was crucified…died…was buried."

When the church ceased being Hebrew and became Greek all was different. Jesus is defined with nouns, emphasis on essence. "God of God, light of light, very God of very God…being of the same substance as the Father."

The earliest church, Hebrew, had no problem insisting Jesus was both human and divine. He walked on the water, stilled the storms, cast out demons and multiplied the bread. Such *acts* evidenced divinity. As the blind man said, "Never since the world began has it been heard that anyone opened the eyes of a man born blind. If this man were not from God he could do nothing." (John 9:32).

In Mark 2, there is no Greek-like statement ("…very God of very God…being of the same substance as the Father"), which convinces his critics that he is making himself equal to God. It is instead an act. Jesus forgave a man his sins and unleashes a thunderbolt! "Why does this man speak thus? It is blasphemy! Who can forgive sins but God alone?" (Mark 2:7)

In like manner, his humanity is observed and confirmed by acts, not by statements about his person or essence: "Jesus, wearied as he was with his journey, sat down beside the well…Jesus said to her, 'Give me a drink'" (John 4:6-7). On the way to Jairus' home to raise his daughter, when jostled, he asks, "Who touched my garments?" (Mark 5:30).

It was only when the church became Greek and thought in nouns that the great Christological struggles began. For the earliest Hebrew church, all one had to do was point to his acts. When the church became Greek, problems arose. It is one thing to point to acts and accept opposites. It is quite another to reconcile opposing essences.

The differences between verb and noun led to enormous differences in many areas. For the Greek, it led to science. Nouns are consistent. Their properties do not change. Water heated becomes vapor. Vapor cooled becomes water. These consistencies can be harnessed and man can control his own destiny (page 24 above). The consequence of that is science, and science breeds humanism, the eventual exaltation of the human spirit. Hellenism is humanism.

Hebrew thought went in the opposite direction. In the Old Testament, there is no science, there is no humanism. God is the actor. God is the *sole* actor. He intervenes and produces unpredictable outcome. The ten plagues, the exodus, Gideon told to reduce his forces to make it clear that it is God's power and not man's that overcome enemies, all these and other examples make it clear that in the old Testament the top rung in the ladder of life is not man but God. Greek thought is science and humanism. Hebrew thought is theology and divine supremacy, absolute and uncompromised. Its emphasis is on the majesty of God, not the capacities of man. In 2 Samuel 6, when the oxen stumbled, Uzzah reached out to protect the ark of the covenant lest it fall. A thoughtful pious deed. For which he was struck dead! And not an eyebrow was raised! Why not? Because God is the ultimate actor. If God wanted the ark to fall, it would fall. If God did not want it to fall, it would not fall. How dare Uzzah presume the prerogatives of God!

It is this supremacy of God and servitude of man, which confronted Epiphanes (page 25 above), which led to Tertullian's caustic rejection of Hellenism, "What has Jerusalem to do with Athens?"

The *major* difference between Hebrew and Greek thought is that Greek thought abhors contradictions. Greek thought is logical, consistent, scientific. If two chemicals are combined, each in a given amount, for a given time, at a set temperature, there is a given consequence. The same experiment performed the next day demands the same result. If there is a difference, an inconsistency, a contradiction, a mistake must have been made. Contradictions or inconsistencies are not tolerated. If proposition A is true and proposition B says the opposite, proposition B must be false. There is a rigid consistency to Greek scientific humanistic thought. Opposites must be eliminated.

Not so for the Hebrew. *Hebrew thought is able to hold opposites together in tension.* When one thinks in terms of verbs, contradictions are allowed to stand. Inconsistencies are acceptable. A person may act one way today, pleasant and smiling, just having won the lottery. The next day, when the money is spent, there is surly sulking. Which is true? Both are true.

Inconsistencies were never a problem for the earliest church. In Mark 10:46 blind Bartimaeus' sight is restored as Jesus is *leaving* Jericho. In Luke 18:35 the event takes place as Jesus *draws near* to Jericho. Matthew agrees with Mark, Jesus was *leaving* Jericho. But Matthew insists it was not one man but two who were healed! (Matt. 20:29). Ours is not the first generation bright enough to see an inconsistency here! The earliest church saw it too. But they *tolerated* it!

The early church not only tolerated contradictions, they actually *created* inconsistencies and contradictions. In Mark 1:11, the voice from heaven spoke to Jesus. The address is in the second person singular. It is Jesus who is told: "*Thou* art my beloved Son, with *thee* I am well pleased." That wording opened the door to the adoptionist theory, that Jesus at that moment became divine, he was being adopted by God and was being informed of that fact, which is why the voice spoke to him!

That was an intolerable interpretation. It had to be corrected. Thus, Matthew 3:17 contradicted Mark 1:11. For Matthew, the voice no longer spoke to Jesus. Instead it spoke to those around Jesus because Jesus already knew who he was. It was *the spectators* who needed to be informed! The original wording was changed; "This is my beloved Son, with whom I am well pleased."

Luke 3:22 allows Mark's original wording to continue. But that is because Luke denies the adoptionist theory in another way, by adding the story of the twelve year old in the temple. Already, then, long before the baptism, Jesus knew God was his Father: "Did you not know that I must be in my Father's house?" (Luke 2:49).

Western scientific thought is logical, consistent, unable to tolerate contradictions. Biblical thought is dialectical, paradoxical, finds truth by holding opposites together in tension.

Jesus was human and divine, not one or the other, both are true.

Holding opposites together in tension, affirming two contradictory statements, is not confined to defining Jesus' person. It is true in every area.

"This is my Father's world," "God causes the rain to fall on the just and unjust." Such phrases confirm the hand of God in the world of nature. Yet nature can be savagely destructive, and when that occurs, it is impossible to trace the savagery back to God and at the same time say that God is love.

Insurance companies can look at hurricanes and floods, all the catastrophes of nature gone berserk, and call them "acts of God." But not the synoptics. For them, storms at sea have to be rebuked and stilled.

Man is free and responsible. Man is helpless. The Bible says both. They are polar opposites but both are true. Despite the inability of the contemporary scene to accept that fact, it is nonetheless observably evident.. Man is both. One day we say "Why did I do that?" An acknowledgement of responsibility. Another day we say, "What got into me?" A confession of helplessness.

Only the Bible has the audacity and the insight to insist that both are true, that man is self-determining and responsible, that man is invaded and capable of catastrophic evil. So Luther, *simul iustus et peccator.*[5]

The philosophers ask, Is man good or evil? The majority say he is good. That was the *only* thing that Plato and Aristotle agreed upon, that Man is good.! That was why both insisted that education was essential, salvatory. Since man was good, show him the right way to walk and he would walk that way.

Plato and Aristotle agreed that man was good, and just about every evaluation of humankind since has agreed. Communism agreed. Man is good. "Give according as you are able, take according to your needs." Since Man is good, he will share when he has plenty. Since Man is good, he will not be greedy and take more than he needs.

Jean Jacques Rousseau, Diderot, Voltaire, all the members of the Enlightenment speak of the noble savage, man is good.

There is of course a minority opinion. Le Marquis de Sade insisted Man was evil, his basic instincts are to rape and to murder. Schopenhauer, the apostle of pessimism, starved himself to death in front of a full table because it was foolish to perpetuate evil Man.

The significant thing is that for Greek western thought, *it is always one or the other*, never both. Man is good, Rousseau. Or man is evil, de Sade. The western mind, grounded in Greek thought, gridlocked with nouns inflexible and unchanging, is incapable of holding opposite together in tension, acknowledging truth in both sides of an argument.

Aristotle and Plato were both wrong. Education is not salvatory. Advanced degrees do not inculcate morality, automatically and universally leading to the *summum bonum* (the highest good). Educate a young thief who steals pennies off the newsstand and he will steal the whole newsstand. So also

---

5. The Latin phrase translated is: simultaneously a saint and a sinner.

wrong were Diderot, and Voltaire, and Marx in Das Capital. Communism collapsed because it had no doctrine of sin.

But de Sade and Schopenhauer are equally unreliable and simultaneously rejectable. Life is too loaded with heroic examples of self-sacrifice and magnificent creations of music and art to insist unilaterally and lamely that man is evil, period.

There *are* two views! But western thought, Aristotelian in nature, the stream in which we swim, is scientifically orientated and, thinking in nouns, is unable to hold opposites together. In Greek western thought, our way of thinking, it is always one or the other. Opposites are rejected.

Only Biblical language has the courage and insight and audacity to insists that it is not one or the other. Both are true, Man is good, Man is evil! We can point to Buchenwald and Auschwitz, and to the ceiling of the Sistine Chapel as well. Both are true.

The difficulty of contemporary Christianity is that we read the Bible with Greek spectacles. We disallow diversity. We insist upon consistency. And thus we miss the splendid richness of Biblical thought.

Our primary need is to think Hebrew. When once we recognize that the genius of Biblical thought is its ability to emphatically affirm polar opposites, we will then be ready to read the Bible intelligently.

Ω

## CHAPTER NINE

# HOLDING OPPOSITES TOGETHER IN TENSION

In the New Testament, opposites can stand. But they cannot stand alone. Each end of the intellectual spectrum is significant. But none are sufficient. Each assertion has to be coupled with and complemented by an opposing axiom. To separate them, to stress one side and ignore or reject the other, is error.

Heresy means false teaching, doctrinal dilution. But heresy comes from a word, which means "truth." Heresy is truth developed in isolation, apart from qualifying counterproposals. It is truth, but only part of the truth, incomplete, a half truth, and hence error.

For example, no honest exegete can dispute the fact that the New Testament has two views of sin, polar opposites, irreconcilable extremes. On the one hand, there is rebellion, disobedience, the refusal to obey God. Spawned in Genesis, it is responsible man in revolt. Adam shaking his thin little fist heavenward and rejecting God's order, "Do not eat of the fruit of this tree."

He eats and then seeks to deny responsibility. He blames it on Eve. She gave me to eat. He goes further. He blames it on God. "It was this woman you gave me who led me astray." Man is responsible, in revolt. Sin is rebellion.

Spawned in Genesis, it is the opening accusation of Isaiah: "Sons have I reared and brought up, but they have rebelled against me" (Isaiah 1:2). Not only spawned in Genesis, not merely the indictment of Isaiah, it is also the core of the Prodigal Son parable. The boy is not "lost." He knows exactly where he is. Where he ought not be. He has left the father's house, he spurned the father's love and ran away from home. And he knew he was responsible, had done wrong: "Father, I have sinned against heaven and before you. I am no longer worthy to be called your son" (Luke 15:18-19).

Yet opposed to that there is Romans 7:15: "I do not understand my own actions. For I do not do what I want, but I do the very thing I hate." Here, sin is no longer an act, it is a condition. Man is no longer responsible. He is helpless, overwhelmed. Sin is personalized, a perverse invasion: "I can will what is right, but I cannot do it...It is no longer I that do it but sin, ("the" sin to be precise. The Greek has the definite article!) which dwells within me" (Romans 7:18, 20). The synoptics paint the same portrait. Helpless man, driven to self-destruction, beating himself with chains, invaded by a Legion, so strong they can take control of one's vocal cords.

Two view of sin, two views of man. Sin is an act for which we are accountable. The Prophet Isaiah and the Baptist in the Bible belt stand shoulder to shoulder saying "Repent...repent!"

But Luther said, Sin is a condition, bondage, an evil enemy we can neither comprehend nor control. Luther was in Rome once, at almost exactly the hour that Michelangelo was painting his masterpieces, yet Luther never acknowledged any of the marvels unfolding around him. Critics assumed the silence was because Luther was a Saxon peasant with manure on his shoes. The fact is, he was silent because he was at the other end of the human spectrum. When Erasmus, intoxicated by the optimistic anthropology of Aristotle reborn, picked up pen in Rotterdam and wrote *The Freedom Of The Will*, Luther in Wittenberg picked up pen and wrote his most powerful work, *The Bondage Of The Will*,[6] in which he insisted that "man is a beast of burden made to be ridden and cannot even choose his own rider." In his explanation of the third article of the creed, Luther wrote "I believe that I cannot by my own reason or strength believe in Jesus…the Holy Spirit has led me and enlightened me." The words are Luther's. The thought was Paul's: "….we do not know how to pray as we ought, but the Spirit himself intercedes for us" (Rom. 8:26).

Both are true. But neither can stand alone. For, separated, they are only half truths, heretical, false and misleading. Stress sin solely as rebellion and you end up putting man at the center of the stage, determiner of his own destiny, baptized humanism, an idea so foreign to Scripture as to be beyond belief. Stress sin solely as a condition of bondage, and the essence of humanity is erased, man is but a mute reactor to alien activity, only a vegetable.

The polar positions are true. But they cannot stand alone. They must be blended. Luther did it in his liturgical confession of sin. "We poor sinners confess unto thee that we are in bondage to sin and cannot free ourselves."

Sin is bondage, man is helpless. But the confession continues: "And we have sinned against thee in thought, word, and deed." Sin is rebellion, and man is responsible. Luther coupled them, that was his genius, able to weld opposites together so that the whole truth was seen. He coupled them but could not

---

6. Martin Luther and others, *The Bondage of the Will* (Grand Rapids: Wm. B. Eerdmans Publishing Company, 1931).

explain them. That is the genius of Biblical thought. Holding irreconcilable opposites together in tension.

On the popular front, in every day discourse, we are able to do the same, hold opposites together in tension. We have a proverb for everything, and sagely say them, never troubled by their contradiction. "Look before you leap." "He who hesitates is lost." "Birds of a feather flock together." "Opposites attract." But when we move from popular concepts into Biblical explanation, a sanctified stupor falls over us and we seem unable to grasp the significance of coupling contradictions.

For example, there are three separate views of suffering in Scripture standing side by side. There is the Old Testament view, the *Principle of Retribution*.

Suffering is from God, a punishment for bad conduct, a consequence of perversity (above, page 14). There is the apocalyptic view, suffering comes from Satan, it is a diabolical attack on the pious, a demonic affliction of the Elect of God (above, pages 25-26). And there is the Johannine view. John returns to the Old Testament view that suffering is from God, but for John it is not punitive but purgative, positive in purpose, a blessing and an advance of God's goodness even if one cannot see that fact in the midst of immediate pain (above, page 53).

There they are, in the Bible, side by side. The Hebrew head was able to hold them all together. But when Christianity left the Hebrew head and walked into the Greek arena, the ability to balance opposites was lost. Today, each of the three views survives, but not in one denomination. Each little arm of the church has opted for one view or another, and, in adopting one view, rejecting the others. Denominational differences exist basically not because of disagreement over a specific text, but rather because one denomination swims in one stream, while other denominations float their theological rafts down another.

Suffering as punishment stemming from God is the basic

building block of the Catholic Church. Anselm asked *Cur Deus Homo*, "Why did God become man?" His answer was that Jesus had come to suffer, to bear our burden. That is why the cross above the altar is never empty. A crucifix, Jesus suffering. That is the primary emphasis of the *Sacre Coeur* (Sacred Heart) motif, Jesus' chest bare and his beating heart exposed. The front wall of the Sistine Chapel hymns not the resurrection but the final judgment. Jesus, with the bronzed arms of a Bolivian Olympic shot-putter, is raising up one arm and calling onto Himself those who were faithful, but with the other, pushing downward into purgatory or perdition those who have strayed. Suffering is salvatory. Fasting is blessed and chastity is better, vows to be taken if you would be a servant.

For Luther, sin was not essentially rebellion requiring punishment. It was slavery, bondage, "For still the ancient foe, whose craft and power are great, doth seek to work us woe. On earth is not his equal." And so the emphasis was not on pious submission to just punishment, but a hope of deliverance, rescue from the oppressive persecutor: "The man of God's own choosing, ask ye who that might be? Christ Jesus it is he, with a word shall overthrow him." For Luther no crucifix. Instead, an empty cross, a liberating savior. And whatever suffering spilled out on God's people, it was not to be seen as punishment but persecution, not from God but from Satan. When Luther was confronted by anguish and enmity, he saw it as Satanic. Suffering was a sign of piety, a confirmation of loyal discipleship (as did Paul – above, page 32): "I must be doing something right, or else why would Satan be attacking me so?"

The third view, suffering is from God but it has a healing purpose with an import, which may elude us now but will one day be seen is the main avenue down, which most of the conservative fundamentalist bodies walk today. When a loved one dies, lipstick is put on the corpse, hands are folded. Praise is poured out, thanksgiving expressed, a memorial service held, and the assurance given that it was the will of God and the departed has gone to a better place. "Thanks be to God."

Each of these is true, but none of them can stand alone. Developed in isolation, sundered from the counter truth, the result is chaos, theological catastrophe.

Of course the Old Testament conviction that suffering is from God and is punitive is true. Disobey the commandments and you pay a price. Drink too much, you ruin your liver and wreck your life. Climb to the top of the church steeple and jump off, you do not break the law of gravity, you break your neck. He who lives by the commandments benefits from the same. He who strays, pays. That is a self-evident fact, obvious to all. Capone died of syphilis.

Yet the fact that suffering is punitive, the result of disobedience to the commandments, cannot stand alone, even when blessed with the imprimatur of Deuteronomy, praised in Psalm One, and spoken ex cathedra. Taken in isolation, the idea that suffering is of God is repulsive. A century ago, when the All Saints Day earthquake in Portugal killed thousands, Voltaire excoriated the Christian God insisting that he who would manufacture such stupendous hurt was unworthy of worship.

Voltaire was not a voice in the wilderness crying out alone. Others of every generation share the same view. Sartre, poor vision, walked into an almond tree and then wrote his semi-serious question, "Who is planting almond trees in my way, forcing me off my path? If suffering comes from God, then Life is Absurd. There is no exit." He struck a cord. He touched a note to which we vibrate. He won the Nobel prize for literature.

So also Albert Camus. He told of the doctor who found a dead rat in front of his door. The same question, "Who is putting dead rats in my way, forcing me off my path?" The dead rat was the carrier of the plague and half the north African village died. The priest summed up Camus' disdain for a God who caused pain by having the priest say the catastrophe was the will of God, punishing a wayward people. When we make God responsible for all suffering, life is both unbearable and absurd. Life is absurd. Camus too, won a Nobel prize. It is impossible to see suffering solely as a punishment from God and yet retain confidence in and affection for such a God.

Insurance companies continue with such rhetoric, by saying in the small print that calamities such as earthquakes and floods, catastrophes of every kind, are "acts of God." But overall, the Old Testament view, which sees suffering as stemming from God who is punishing man for his misdeeds, is so repulsive that it has all by disappeared. When Pat Robertson dared to venture that the anomalies of nature, destructive tsunamis, were God's punishment for sin, even his fellow fundamentalists drew back and shuddered.

The apocalyptic view, too, taken in isolation, cannot stand alone. At this level, Bultmann is right. Modern man is simply too sophisticated to accept the antiquated idea that a red-pajama-clad ogre armed with a pitchfork stabs us in the pants every time we sin is simply silly. The idea is cartooned away, laughed at. And so we assume that this view too is to be set aside. Suffering cannot be ascribed to God, the idea is repulsive. And Suffering can be assigned to Satan, that is antiquated and outmoded. At least in this instance, contemporary thought repeats Jesus and casts out demons! Instead of seeing sickness as Satan we give disease a Greek or a Latin name and call it a virus, as if that answered the agony of sickness and pain!

Two of the three Biblical views as to the origin or purpose of suffering are set aside. Old Testament thought, that suffering is divine punishment, is spurned as repulsive. And the apocalyptic insistence that suffering is of Satan is quaint and old-fashioned, as extinct as a mastodon.

That leaves only the Johannine view that suffering is indeed from God, but it is not punitive. It is instead purposeful or purgative. It has a hidden promise of goodness not seen now but which will be revealed later.

That is all we have left! We live with that anemic and weak view, that insipid explanation, in and of itself insulting and obscene! We actually accept it!

We salve ourselves with the pietistic nonsense that there is a purpose to pain and it is all part of God's plan. That is self-deception. When our life has been ruptured, a loved one ripped away, a mate of fifty years wrenched out of our life leaving us numbed, when a sixteen year old son is buried even before his life began, when the fabric of our life is shredded, our dreams dashed, our aspirations turned to ashes, and we say it is the will of God, shame on us. Death is an enemy, the last great enemy (1 Cor. 15:26). Jesus entered into humanity that "through death he might destroy him who has the power of death, that is, the devil" (Heb. 2:14).

The three different Biblical views of suffering are contradictory. They are at odds one with the others. They are irreconcilable. Any one of them by itself is unacceptable. But *together*, holding opposites together in tension, at last an acceptable explanation is at hand!

Suffering *can* be a just punishment of a holy God. Or suffering *can* be a sweet release of a loving Father calling his child gently homeward, relieving them of the obscene pains of cancer. Or suffering can be what Paul called it and what Luther called it – an attack of the evil one.

In its infancy, startled spectators looked at the warriors of Jesus and in awed admiration labeled them οι την οικου-μενην αναστατωσαντες, "world-turners-upside-downers," "those who have set the habitable world in confusion!" (Acts 17:6). If that ultimate impact is ever to be retained, if ever again the church is once more to have such an astounding impact as it had in those early days when they were labeled "world-turners-upside-downers" *the church must once again learn to think Hebrew. It must be able to hold opposites together as does Scripture.*

In the earliest church the multiplicity of views were fused into a whole because the earliest church was Hebrew, able to think dialectically. Later, when the church became Greek in thought, the ability to hold opposites together in tension continued, but only because there were different denominations emphasizing polar extremes.

That was the promise when the Ecumenical Era began, that at last the whole symphony of God could be heard. If one head could not hold all these ideas together, at least every note could at last be heard when all of the denominations set aside their rivalries and shared together! Perhaps as Methodist and Lutheran, Catholic and Episcopal, gathered in conference the full symphony of Biblical thought was to be heard, rather than the cacaphonic monotone of single denominational emphases. Ecumenism was pregnant with promise.

John XXIII welcomed dialogue with "our separated brethren." Separated, yes, but brotherhood recognized at last! Catholic would hear the Methodist emphasis, underlining not simply the suffering of Jesus, but insisting upon the repentance of man. Presbyterians could talk of predestination, the omnipotent activity of God who controlled all, offering such a view as an alternative or corrective to the Baptist insistence that all of salvation depended on me, my faith, real faith, an answer to an altar call.

The age of ecumenicism offered great promise. It appears, however, to be fading, to have forfeited its power to renew. We are too polite. Timidity has prevailed. Rather than a Lutheran forcefully asserting his insistence that sin is bondage and man unable, instead of a Pentecostal insisting that sin was rebellion and man had to surrender, instead of each denominational position being championed and shared so that all might be heard, instead we are too polite. In the conversations, we seek out and stress not our differences but what we have in common. We end up with the lowest common denominator.

The church will once again be the robust force energizing lives and erasing pain when once it learns to think Hebrew, recognizing that opposites are to be held in tension, when it recognizes that indeed there are cleavages, Mark does not say the same thing as John, the fourth gospel does not agree with Paul. But each of these opposites is laden with truth, not to be pitted one against the other, but welded anew into a world-altering crescendo.

Ω

# ABOUT THE AUTHOR

James Kallas has led an impressive life. During World War II he enlisted in the U.S. Navy at age fourteen. When they learned he was too young and discharged him, he went to college and became an outstanding athlete, later a professional football player. He began his ministerial career as a missionary in the Cameroun, West Africa, later a professor of New Testament at California Lutheran, then a College, now a University, and finally as President of Dana College, Blair, NE.

His work at restoring Dana College to robust health led to his being knighted by the Queen of Denmark (Dana was founded a century ago by Danish immigrants). But it was that stay in Africa which first brought him to the attention of serious theology.

While still in his twenties, SPCK published his first book (*The Significance Of The Synoptic Miracles,* London 1961. Reprinted by Sunrise Reprints, Woodinville, WA). Its debut was impressive. Apart from a myopic comment in *The Church Times of London* which labeled it "a superficial book, irritating in its narrow dogmatism…remarkably expensive," the international reviews were laudatory. *The Baptist Times* insisted, "This book opens up horizons as yet insufficiently explored." *The British Weekly* commended it for its profound evangelical commitment" and concluded that the book "cannot be ignored by any who would wrestle with the miracles." And *The Anglican Of Australia* after praising the "fiery urgency" and comparing the author to Schweitzer went on to insist that this was "the best short book…since Principal Cairns produced 'The Faith That Rebels' in 1923…a rare book which will produce much thought." And *The Expository Times* called it a "robust even robustious affirmation expressed with much eloquence and many telling phrases, that in the miracles we see God establishing His control over the powers of evil…It is a legitimate point of view, and it is well to face it."

Superb reviews, but the book fell flat. It never sold. Because it appeared at the same moment that Bultmann's sixteen page article, referred to elsewhere, appeared. Bultmann was insisting that the demonic had to excised, erased out of the New Testament, or the church would lose its audience. Kallas was at the other end of the spectrum, insisting that if Jesus' victory over Satan was erased, the audience might be salvaged, but there would be nothing to tell them. The message would be lost! Bultmann's proposal proved far more attractive. Demythologizing became the norm, and Kallas' work was shuffled off into the shadows.

But now, fifty years later, two things are clear. First of all, the evidence is in. Despite its lack of broad sales a half century ago, that book altered the flow of New Testament literature. Before he wrote, an acknowledgement of the dominance of the demonic in the New Testament did not exist. Bultmann rejected Satan but Bultmann was not St. George who slew the dragon. He was merely a pallbearer at the funeral. In one sense, demythologizing was unnecessary. Even before the sixteen page article, Satan had been set aside. Not denied, just ignored. *The Significance Of The Synoptic Miracles* ended that. For the first time serious theologians entered the path first paved by Kallas and began to at least accept if not endorse the impact of Satan on New Testament thought.

The second thing which became clear has been the bankruptcy of Bultmann's program of demythologizing. Kallas' dire warning that following said Pied Piper programs would lead to paralysis and impotence have come to be true. Protestant theology today has lost its anchor. It has no absolutes.

Adrift, it is no longer able to arouse and inspire, strengthen, and enrich.

The contribution of his earlier work is expanded in this his latest and perhaps last writing. What was a limited earlier statement, explaining the impact of apocalyptic only in respect to the miracles, has now been expanded to cover the full sweep of the New Testament. What Kallas said so pungently about the miracles of Mark has now been broadened to include all the motifs of the synoptics, plus all of the letters of Paul! That is one contribution.

The second contribution of this present work which may eventually have an impact even greater than the making of apocalyptic the new benchmark, Kallas proceeds to show how John set aside such ideas, but concludes that these polar opposites have <u>both</u> to be embraced if the full vibrancy of the gospel message is to inspire and strengthen and enrich anew. His insistence on the dialectical or paradoxical nature of Scripture, that opposites must be held together in tension, has never before been approached.

Ω

# References Cited

Bultmann, Rudolf. *Theology of the New Testament.* New York: Scribner, 1951.

Dodd, C. H. *The Parables of the Kingdom.* London: Nisbet & Co. Ltd., 1935.

Fuller, Reginald H. *Kerygma and Myth.* London,: S. P. C. K., 1953.

Hunter, Archibald Macbride. *Interpreting Paul's Gospel.* Philadelphia: Westminster Press, 1955.

Luther, Martin, Henry Cole, Edward Thomas Vaughan, and Henry Atherton. *The Bondage of the Will.* Grand Rapids: Wm. B. Eerdmans Publishing Company, 1931.

MacGregor, G.H.C. "Principalities and Powers." *New Testament Studies* Vol.1 (1954-55).

Manson, William. "Principalities and Powers." *Bulletin of Studiorum Novi Testamenti Societas* III, no. 8 (1952).

Schweitzer, Albert, and W. Montgomery. *The Quest of the Historical Jesus: A Critical Study of Its Progress from Reimarus to Wrede.* New York: Macmillan, 1950.

Stewart, James. "On a Neglected Element in New Testament Thought." *Scottish Journal Of Theology* Vol. 4, (1951).

# The Significance of the Synoptic Miracles by James Kallas

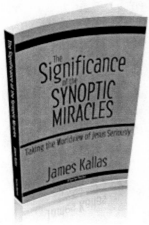

This book was written as a protest against the demythologizing tendencies which characterize so much contemporary theology: it questions the assumption that the New Testament can be understood in terms other than its own. In particular the author is dissatisfied with the interpretation of the miracles that such theology can give. In his submission a theology which acknowledges, and then fails to take account of, or strips away altogether, the demonological thought–world into which the miracle stories are woven, results in only a partial estimate of their significance. Here the miracles are restored to their context, seen in perspective as historical happenings, and considered in relation to Jesus' central theme of the Kingdom.

In this book, written a half century ago, Kallas flew full force into the face of the prevailing way of interpreting the New Testament. While scholarship as a whole was convinced that the New Testament had to be modernized, stripped of its archaic and medieval language or the church would lose it audience, Kallas argued in the opposite direction, insisting that while a rewrite of the New Testament would salvage our audience, we would have nothing to tell them for the gospel would have been emasculated. Fifty years of flaccid flawed pap has proven him right and has demanded a reprint of this his first book.